MW00878487

What Can I Do?

Assurance That You Can Do It

Charlotte C. Chabuka

ISBN 978-1-64191-596-0 (paperback)
ISBN 978-1-64191-597-7 (digital)

Christian Faith Publishing, Inc.
832 Park Avenue
Meadville, PA 16335
www.christianfaithpublishing.com

Printed in the United States of America

This book is dedicated to my sister Lillian B. Chabuka, who has struggled for more reasons than one to consistently pursue her God given gifts and talents, and to the children of God who are still wondering, "When is it going to be my turn?"

I didn't have the time
but I made the time
I didn't have the knowledge
but I did what I knew
I didn't have the support
but I learned to support myself
I didn't have the confidence
but the confidence came with results
I had a lot going against me
but I had enough going for me
I had plenty of excuses
but I chose not to use any of them

—Unknown Author

Contents

⟿∿⟿∘ᒯ᠗ᒧᒦᒧ᠗ᒷ∘⟿∿⟿

Acknowledgments

I AM FOREVER THANKFUL TO the Almighty God who has been my hope and strength all of my days. I bless his name for his grace to give me this opportunity to reach multitudes through this book. I never imagined writing books, but through him, imaginations can become a reality.

I am grateful for my family. My dad, Bedford Kaseya, who consistently persisted and continues to pray for my success and well-being.

My brother Collins Chabuka to my sisters Lillian Chabuka, Emelda Chabuka Mumba, and Beauty Chabuka. I honor God for their encouragement and believing in me, praying for me, and cheering me on. There's no other family I would have chosen.

To my pastor, Pastor Bryant Townsend and his wife Lady Tanisha Townsend. I thank you for constantly and consistently reminding me of my gifts and talents, for speaking life into my endeavors and for watching over my soul as my spiritual parents.

To my friend Desiree Lanier, I will never forget how you always lifted my spirit when I was down. How you encouraged me, prayed for me and with me on this very long journey. To you my friend, I say thank you and may God bless you beyond your imagination.

To my parents away from home, my mother Judy Tripp and my very own papa John Tripp. I thank you for your prayers, words of encouragement, unexpected gifts, and for always wanting nothing but the best for me. Oh yes, and for them priceless pound cakes. Yummy!

To my spiritual mother and pastor, Pastor Jacqueline Teresa Thomas, I know you were sent to me from up above. We have so much in common I can almost say, "God gave me another mother." I believe I am the daughter you never had. With tremendous joy, I thank you for loving me as your own. I thank you for your prayers, support, gifts, and for entertaining my spoilt brat mentality. I love you, and there's nothing you can do about it.

To my friends Dr. Tarisai Githu, Daniel Appah, Iyare, Joyce Abatey Gakwa, Dr. and Mrs. Acha, Mr. and Mrs. Dr. Ngounu, Mr. and Mrs. Kamga, Arnold Nakaha, Kevin Nakaha, Benjamin Nartey, The Goldies, Enobong Archibong, Stephanie Benao, Mbuwa Stepanie Lungu, Mr. and Mrs. Fisher, Isaac and Paulina Kwarteng, Jaqueline King, Lacey Haggan, Esther Nthuli, Muma Prisca Kafula, Sylvia Ofori, Muriel Deah, Dr. Andrew Sobers, Gertrude Wonmel, Britany O'Meara Stanley Nwoke, Susan Ikeagwu, Obasie Ikeagwu, Ok Ikeagwu, Evaristo Soler, Monica Fabbi, George Watson II, Kathleen Archer, Karen Bain, Sara Orr, Evans Manu, Mame Bocar Ba, Zoe Ann Olson, Linda and Alan Bosio, Ana Chavez, Isa Ntakarutimana, Ms. Bobbie, and my entire church family.

To you all, I thank you for your support. Thank you for your prayers, encouragement, love, and time.

All of you contributed to me in more ways than one. May God richly bless you.

Introduction

⁓⦁⧫⦁⧫⦁⧫⦁⧫⦁⧫⦁⦁⧫⧫⧫⦁⦁⧫⦁⧫⦁⧫⦁⧫⦁⧫⧫⦁⧫⦁⧫⦁⧫⦁⦁⧫⦁⧫⦁⧫⦁⧫⦁⧫⦁⧫⦁⧫⦁⧫⦁⧫⦁⧫

THIS BOOK WILL TAKE YOU on a journey like no other. It is intended to compel you to find and use the power you already have within you. This is one of many techniques you can apply to your ministry, education, marriage, sports, business, career, etc. This information is applicable in real time.

We are always waiting for that perfect moment to be able to do what we know we ought to do. Let's embark on a journey that will enlighten us and show us the time is now, you don't have to wait any longer. You can move in the direction you want to go with what you have right now.

There are many times in our lives we push back on fulfilling our calling. We get comfortable saying things such as "I'll help when I get more time" or "I'll start giving back when I become a millionaire." I'll start pursuing my dream when I graduate. I'll start enjoying my life when my kids are grown and gone. I'll open that business when I get more money. We all have different reasons why we don't do or don't have what we want. The reasons are endless, I am sure we can all relate.

The most common reason I have heard, which I am guilty of myself, is "I don't have the money or the time." Most of the time we are waiting for something that can only happen if we ourselves make the first move.

The question you need to ask yourself is "What do I have right now?" "What is it that I can do?" while you wait to get more money, to get that business started, lose the weight, or get that degree. The tools you need to make it possible to get to where you want to be spiritually, mentally, financially, and in relationships are within your reach waiting for you to respond. Look within yourself and dig deep. You know what your passion is! Whatever popped up on your mind is exactly what it is. You wonder, *How can I do it?* Write it down and get a blueprint of what you would want it to look like. How would you like it to bless you and others? A business/service is waiting to be birthed with that very idea that you have on your mind. The world is waiting to hear from you. And your life is looking for that transformation you have been waiting for.

Shall I Pursue?

1

PROVERBS 3:5 TEACHES US TO trust in the Lord at all times and lean not on your own understanding and acknowledge him in all your ways. It is quite clear that you can't always trust your own thoughts, especially if there are negative. Periodically a pleasant thought may cross your mind and send out emotions of excitement, only to be discouraged by the little voice that tells you, "You can't do that, you don't have the money, resources, knowledge, or experience." Instead of entertaining that negative voice, ask yourself, "Could this be an opportunity?" If so, read about it, watch videos about it, talk to people who have done it before, for nothing is new under the sun.

It is your responsibility to monitor your thoughts. Monitor how often you think about something, how one thing or another reminds you of a specific idea. When you realize your passion for it, do some research on that subject.

The more educated you are about your passion, talent, or desire, the closer you are. The more familiar you become, the more confidence you'll develop. The amount of work and effort required to move forward may demotivate you, but remember nothing good comes without hard work. The more competition your area of interest has, the more work you must put into your product/service to make it unique and more desirable than the others.

It will be important that you acknowledge God in all your ways. There's nothing more comforting than the assurance of God. When you ask God if it is time to pursue a project, and he says yes—and you know without a shadow of doubt that he said yes—no matter how the going gets, you always have confirmation to fall back on. Waiting on God is not always easy, but I can guarantee you that its always worth the wait. He makes all things better, he makes all things new, and everything he does supersedes man's mind, timing, and expectation.

Your talent can become a resource for you and others. By this, I mean you can always find healing, love, joy, and peace pursuing what you know God has called you to do. At the same time, other people can be the benefactors of your purpose. Working or using your talent is nothing anyone can ever compensate you for what it's worth. It's your God-given gift. Only you can best operate in it. It is priceless. If not put into action, it's wasting away, but when in action, it unfolds purpose and can be a stepping-stone to greater.

Doing what we are created to do is our reasonable service and fulfillment for our authentic reason for existence.

The question "Shall I pursue?" speaks to different parts of your mind and physical being. To be able to ask the question means that there is an idea floating in your mind. There might be an idea that has been revealed to you through prayer and/or by revelation, and sometimes it's just a vision or a dream coming into manifestation.

Sometimes people encourage us and help birth ideas into existence. We may feel the task at hand is impossible, but it will remain impossible until we make that first step.

Nevertheless when you get to the point where you are wondering whether to pursue or not, it means you are at the decision door of a new journey. You are one decision away from making a life-changing decision or not. And sometimes you are really at the verge of making that decision of either going forward and pursuing the promised land or are signing up to walk around in the wilderness.

The land of milk and honey exists, and it is a land available to all who are determined to be a part of it and to all who seek it diligently. The question "Shall I pursue?" will reappear in many areas of your life. Sometimes it's a matter of should I go or not, should I move or not, should I ask or not, should I do it or not, will it work or not, will I be successful or not. All these questions are legitimate, and making any of these decisions can be one of the scariest positions to be in. Some decisions are simpler than others; unfortunately, some may be a matter of life and death. Some decisions will lead you to unplug from a world you are familiar with. A place of discomfort can be a place that allows you to see yourself in a whole different strength and a whole new identity. It allows you to see things from a whole different perspective.

Unbelievably, the fun part about pursuing something is the fear. Most of the times we can get consumed in fear of the unknown. The fear of not knowing the outcome can be discouraging in making a decision or even pursuing a goal. Remember though, that the "go ahead" light has been on for a long time waiting on you to move. When you finally overcome your fear of the unknown, then will you be able to pursue.

I remember a time when God gave me an answer to prayer, and without a shadow of a doubt, I believed I heard him and trusted him to work things out for me. In that instance, I got comfortable and relaxed, waiting for God to work it out for me. The more I waited, the more the situation changed and looked far from the promise. At some point, I decided this was never going to happen. I made up my mind that it was over and tried to convince myself otherwise. This was not easy because every now and then, I kept on thinking about the promise. Years went by, and I would still think about it. Finally, I started understanding why it took so long to come together; I started seeing God's hand assemble the pieces, and as difficult as the process was, it was more than comforting to start seeing the promise come together. I am sharing this because we all have promises that God has given to us, promises he has given us directly or has spoken to us through someone else. These promises have not come to life yet because either we don't believe or have not taken the time to pursue them. The good news about receiving a promise from God, or what I sometimes call the green light (the go-ahead), is that it is not dependent upon your attitude. However, the position of your heart and mind is important because the quicker you snap out of your doubt, pity party, fear, or whatever you want to call that obstacle, the sooner you will see his word coming to life. The promise always waits on you as God has already put the master piece together.

I spent so much time questioning instead of waiting on God to prove himself. There's nothing wrong with wanting God to show himself out because after all he is God and he does wonders. If you believe in your heart you've heard him, chances are that you probably did. God is not man; he does not lie, and whatever he says or directs you to do—whether you do it or not—will still be open for you to do when you are ready. There will be times when you are ready, and when a word comes through, it will be that confirmation you need to pursue. In the case of when you are not ready, a seed is planted on your mind and no matter how much you doubt it or try to shake it off, it's still stuck on the back your mind and God always has a way to bring it back to the forefront of your memory. In fact, God is on your side and is ready to walk you through the process the moment you are ready to do the work.

There are many times we feel inadequate and we tend to say things such as "This is not for me" or "I would never be able to accomplish that!" Whichever way you may look at it, you're right. By yourself, it's not possible, but with God all things are possible, and that's why you must keep your eyes on God. More often than not, instructions from God almost never make sense. We are no match to God's wisdom. One way to overcome doubt is to continue praying. It's also safe to say, "God help me understand my role is in this mission." At the end of the day, just trust God, if not for any other reason for the fact that he is God. After all he is the creator of creation.

Yes, You May Pursue

2

Be led by the Holy Spirit, by revelation, and not by thought. If God didn't say it, don't do it, it will derail you. Anything that God did not plant will be uprooted simply because it does not have a strong foundation. God has given each one of us the ability to reap what we sow. The success or the growth of your seed will largely depend on your foundation. Through Scripture, we know that the only house that will stand the storm is the house that has the foundation of the rock.

> *[T]herefore whosoever heareth these sayings of mine, and doeth them, I will liken him unto a wise man, which built his house upon the rock: And the rain descended, and the floods came, and the winds blew, and beat upon that house; and it fell not: for it was founded upon the rock. (Matthew 7:24–25)*

Once God says yes, the sky then becomes the limit. Be very aware that you will face opposition from both the seen and unseen world.

> *For we wrestle not against flesh and blood, but against principalities, against powers, against the rulers of the darkness of this world, against spiritual wickedness in high places. Wherefore take unto you*

*the whole armour of God, that ye may be able to
withstand in the evil day, and having done all, to
stand. Stand therefore, having your loins girt about
with truth, and having on the breastplate of righ-
teousness; And your feet shod with the preparation
of the gospel of peace; Above all, taking the shield
of faith, wherewith ye shall be able to quench all
the fiery darts of the wicked. And take the helmet of
salvation, and the sword of the Spirit, which is the
word of God: Praying always with all prayer and
supplication in the Spirit, and watching thereunto
with all perseverance and supplication for all saints.*
(Ephesians 6:12–18, KJV)

You will have to fully clothe yourself, for God will be your strength. Friends, family, loved ones can become stumbling blocks. Remember that you are the carrier of your vision, the masterpiece of your plan; without you, that seed God planted in you does not exist unless you nurture it into a plant.

Odds may come against you, but keep on pushing, keep on pressing, and surely your vision will come to fruition. There's no better source of confidence other than knowing that God has your back and your front. If God be for you, who can be against you?

Be cautioned: just because you know God told you to pursue doesn't make it easy, but it sure helps making it believable.

When God speaks into your life, it sometimes takes time before you can start moving. I knew I thought about writing a book, and even though I didn't do anything to pursue it, it was tucked away in my memory that I was an author. When I started to write this book, I thought I wrote it simply because I was bored. I was trying to keep busy. I was determined not to make my mind the devil's workshop.

Surprisingly, as I continued to write, God revealed to me that I had a word of encouragement for someone.

I remember sometime in December of 2012 when I had just moved to Boise, Idaho. My pastor had asked me if I wrote books. I simply responded, "No."

He said to me, "You should get with my wife because she writes books." I didn't pay much attention simply because I didn't think I was a writer. Two years later, a friend of mine called me and told me about a dream he had; he mentioned that I had written and published a bestseller. This revelation took me back to the question my pastor once asked me. I was propelled to write this book, but I procrastinated for a total of four years from the time my pastor had asked. It was not until two years after my friend's dream that I started writing this book. By this time, I remembered that God had already given me the title to this book two years prior.

As I started to write, it came to memory that I was already working on being an author from the time I was younger. As a teenager, I wrote a lot of poetry. Suddenly I was awakened to the writer's spirit within me. This is my first book, and as I write, I don't know who or where it is going to be published, how much it is going to cost me, or the steps to take before it is certified fit for public view ha-ha-ha. All I have working for me right now is the assurance from God that I should pursue. At this time, I am convinced to continue writing, and as I do so, God is continuously opening doors and straightening crooked paths for my next step.

As I shared with a group of friends about my vision for this book, one mentioned that he had written and published two books, and he extended his knowledge in how to get my book ready for publishing. You see, as I started to pursue my vision, God had already laid out a plan and all I had to do was move and align myself with the plan.

When we finally venture into a project that seemed difficult to start, we slowly begin to realize our potential and capabilities. I noticed I was very good at procrastinating and making excuses for procrastinating. When someone tried to challenge me about my excuses, I would become defensive. As a matter of fact, I would be upset and ask them to be concerned about their own problems. Deep down I knew they were looking out for me, but having someone point at your weaknesses is never comfortable. I could not make any progress until I said to myself, *"No more excuses, no more complaining.*

Never say you can't. Always keep a positive attitude. Always remember to be grateful for what you already have."

Identify your weaknesses and deal with them. It's only until you deal with them head on can change take place. Also it helps to listen to people around you; they sometimes see more than you can about yourself. This may be positive or negative. And it may be something wrongfully portrayed about you; either way, it calls for change. Until you see it from their point of view, your progress may be delayed even more.

Now I don't mean that you change to please people, but be open enough to apply change in areas that you probably know need that change. A simple way to identify problems that need work could be flashpoints you have heard family members and close peers complain about. This does not mean that all complaints need change. You be the judge of your own behavior. If change doesn't take place, it will either make you or break you. The choice is yours. In the same respect, they may point out something positive about you; if you take heed to that, you may birth something new or master the art of your gift.

Your Words Are Working
for You or against You

3

THE BIBLE SAYS THAT LIFE and death is in the power of the tongue. It is all in the words that come out of your mouth.

> *Death and life are in the power if the tongue: and they that love it shall eat the fruit thereof.* (Proverbs 18:21, NKJV)

> *But the tongue can no man tame; it is an unruly evil, full of deadly poison. Therewith bless we God, even the Father; and therewith curse we men, which are made after the similitude of God. Out of the same mouth proceedeth blessing and cursing. My brethren, these things ought not so to be. Doth a fountain send forth at the same place sweet water and bitter?* (James 3:3–11, NKJV)

The tongue is believed to be one of the smallest organs in the body, but yet it carries so much power and control over the entire body. If you have read, the tongue cannot be tamed. What does this mean? Two things come to my mind:

1. That there is no method to get the tongue under control, and there's nothing you can do about it. That is scary. Watch your mouth now!
2. What we speak out into the atmosphere cannot be taken back.

The end of verse 10 says *"My brethren these things ought not to be so,"* and verse 11 says *"Doth a fountain send forth at the same place sweet water and bitter water."*

What kind of words do you want to flow out of your fountain?

Some words curse you, but some bless you. Some curses have been activated in people's lives in the name of jokes. May I remind you the Holy Spirit's purpose is not to distinguish the difference between a joke and what was really meant to be said.

"[S]o shall my word be that goeth forth out of my mouth: it shall not return unto me void, but it shall accomplish that which I please, and it shall prosper in the thing whereto I sent it" (Isaiah 55:11, NKJV).

The Scripture says that when we speak, the word spoken will go out to accomplish that which it has been instructed to do. It is a mandate. Therefore, we need to be very careful what we utter, whether it be out of frustration or emotion. There is a real devil walking around to and fro, looking for someone to devour. And in the midst of negativity, he is ever present.

God says whatsoever negative or positive, faith or unbelief, when you lose it on earth, it will be loosed in heaven.

Whatsoever is bound on earth is also bound in heaven. I believe we lose and we bind using our words. Therefore, it's important to speak life into the different areas of our lives.

The devil cannot read your mind. Everything the devil uses against you he has heard from your mouth or someone else's mouth. He is also a master of trickery, using trial and error.

I've come to understand that whatever you put out will come back to you—good attitude, bad attitude, money, greed, hate, anger, love, joy, laughter, peace, and kindness. If you give out any of these things, however you do it, you will get back exactly that. It's like the analogy that if you plant an apple tree don't expect to reap oranges. Go figure.

If you don't like some things in your life, it starts with how you think, then what you say, and eventually what you do. All the things you have achieved can be traced back to your words and your thought process.

> *In the beginning was the Word, and the Word was with God, and the Word was God. The same was in the beginning with God. All things were made by him; and without him was not anything made that was made. In him was life; and the life was the light of men. And the light shineth in darkness; and the darkness comprehended it not.* (John 1:1–5, NKJV)

When God decided to create the world, he spoke into the atmosphere and he said, *"Let there be light."* And there was light. What does light do? Light overcomes darkness. You can recreate by your spoken word. So let the light be manifested by your words and make sure the word works for you and not against you. Speak the things that you want to see even when your situation looks worse and does not match what is coming out of your mouth. The more you speak it, the more it becomes, and the more it becomes, the more you believe. The reason most of our prayers don't come to pass is because we don't believe what we are saying.

I urge you speak positively even though you have unbelief. I would rather you speak positively into your own life or someone else's life instead of exercising negative energy.

The exciting part of what comes out of your mouth is when you ask or speak, ask in Jesus's name, for he promised us that

"And whatsoever ye shall ask in my name, that will I do, that the Father may be glorified in the Son.¹⁴If ye shall ask any thing in my name, I will do it" (John 14:13–14, NKJV).

This scripture is very personal to me because it's such a promise that God is literally emphasizing the truth in this method. Every time I read this scripture, I hear God telling me, "Try it and prove it for yourself." This is true and it works, and if it doesn't, it has nothing to do with the Word because the Word itself is true, tried, and tested.

> *For verily I say unto you, that whosoever shall say*
> *unto this mountain, be thou removed, and be thou*
> *cast into the sea; and shall not doubt in his heart,*
> *but shall believe that those things which he saith*
> *shall come to pass; he shall have whatsoever he saith.*
> *Therefore I say unto you, what things soever ye*
> *desire, when ye pray, believe that ye receive them,*
> *and ye shall have them.* (Mark 11:23–24, NKJV)

As easy as this scripture reads, it's exactly what we have been instructed to say. The prerequisite is your belief. I believe it's the missing part for most of us. Yeah, yeah, I know sometimes it seems impossible to believe. As for me, I choose to say it anyway, even when my eyes don't seem to trace the change I'm causing in the atmosphere.

When we go before the Lord, we must be as bold as a lion. We need to make sure that any forms of doubt and little voices of the enemy are completely muted. You can always ask God to help your unbelief. The Bible says with the heart we believe, and with the mouth we confess.

Speak with conviction and confess with expectation. We must expect everything we decree.

One important lesson I recently learned is when you don't know or have no confidence in Jesus, you cannot command your sphere of influence, but if you know him, you know that he is seated on the right-hand side of the throne pleading for you.

> *Now unto him that is able to do exceeding abun-*
> *dantly above all that we ask or think, according to*
> *the power that worketh in us,*
> *Unto him be glory in the church by Christ*
> *Jesus throughout all ages, world without end. Amen.*
> (Ephesians 3:20–21, NKJV)

Part of accomplishing the answers to your prayers is knowing that God does more than your mind can take or understand. So the same way as we command evil to stay away, we can command positive things into our lives. Let the Word work for you.

Some situations or circumstances have come about in response to your call. Be mindful of the energy around you. As Christians, I know we believe that no weapons formed against us shall prosper; however, God didn't say the weapons wouldn't be formed. How are they formed? Some of them are formed by your words. Such as "Life is hard," "Between me and poverty is…" These are some of the words/phrases we use to corner ourselves. Be careful not to be ensnared by our own words.

Some of the things we are still fighting today were spoken into our lives long before by an angry parent, upset friends, angry strangers, grandmas, and grandpas.

"*Say unto them, as truly as I live, saith the Lord, as ye have spoken in mine ears, so will I do to you*" (Numbers 14:28, NKJV).

Some of the blessed people you see around you are blessed because of their praying generations, parents, grandparents, praying friends, and associates; someone was interceding for them. As we speak, we must be mindful of what we are saying. The main point is that your vision can be achieved through your words, actions, and through prayer; these could be simple words that edify your own soul.

My grandma once said to me when I was age ten that I was business-minded and was destined to travel the world. My middle name means "one who works hard," almost like a workaholic. Looking back, I have traveled quite a bit, I am business-minded, but I never imagined that I would one day be labeled a workaholic. By the way, I just found out not too long ago what my middle name means after months and months of pressuring my dad. My grandma finally told me.

This goes to show you that just because your mind cannot see what has been laid out for you doesn't mean that it won't play out. God already knows your end from your beginning, and he had it in mind before he placed you in your mother's womb.

Believe me your miracle already exists—it's up to you to claim it.

What you speak over your life starts working for you immediately after utterance. It starts shifting your atmosphere to make room for it, and it won't stop until it is accomplished. God promises us in Jeremiah that he will see to it that his word is performed.

As you take charge in speaking your vision into existence, continue to pray for the success of your vision. Be assured challenging days will come around, and when you don't have the strength to speak, you will still be covered by your words when you had the strength to speak.

I have been speaking twins into my life, and even though I have not yet been blessed with a husband, I have enough courage to speak it into my life because it is a desire. I'm sure you can't wait to hear about the outcome when my husband and I are blessed. I will be sure to tell you all about it in one of my many books to come. Although this is my first book, I already have dreams of my second. Don't wait to see the smoke in order for you to know there is a fire. What do I mean by that? I don't have to wait to see book number two in order to know it exists. I don't have to be married first in order to speak into my own marriage. I don't have to say, "I do" to transform my mind into a helpmate. I don't have to hold my twins first before I can speak into their lives, and I certainly don't have to wait for my grandkids to speak a blessing into their lives.

One of the things I love about God is that you are never too late or too early to speak. What we speak into existence at any point in life hovers in the atmosphere and awaits to align with God's calendar. In due season, we reap.

The power of your success, healing, health, successful ministry, marriage, relationship, or whatever you need is in your mouth.

Every day whichever word you speak, you are making a decision to move either toward greatness or towards obscurity. And remember when God tells you to pursue something, you have just as much power to speak it into existence. The truth is your petition depends on what he said to you. There's no greater confidence than the one that comes with knowing you are in the right spirit and your prayer is aligned with the will of God.

It is very important to align your thoughts and words with God's. That's why sometimes when I get into the "woe is me" moment. I make talking to God a priority more than I do to others. I complain and cry out to God, then I later share with my friends. Now I have heard that complaining can cause delays. With that said, I find myself announcing to God, "I'm not complaining" right before I say what I want to say. Sometimes I proceed with saying something like "I'm sorry if I am complaining, but this thing right here hurts," and I cry out to him. The truth is if you can do away with complaining, it is better and safer for you. Who wants to wallow in a situation if complaining has a negative effect?

All in all, make sure that whatever comes out of your mouth works for you and not against you. And since we read that we cannot tame the tongue, I urge you not to open your mouth, especially when you are upset. I can't stress how important it is to speak positively into your life and the lives of others. Most of us have heard the saying "If you have nothing nice to say, don't say anything." It's a good principle to abide by.

Chances are that all those negative things you had to say about your parents, wife, husband, kids, or loved ones meant no harm. You were just upset and now look at how those words begin to manifest right before your eyes. However, the same mouth that spoke those words into existence has as much power to cancel some of the negativity. Why would you put yourself through all this pressure? Wouldn't it be easier to be nicer to yourself and others? I'm sure you would agree that it takes less energy to be nicer than it does to be mean. Use your words wisely, and remember speaking positive words are a fundamental tool to help you move, start, and finish your project.

You Can Do Anything but
You Can't Do Everything

4

"I CAN DO ALL THINGS through Christ who strengthens me."

Yes, we can do all things through Christ who strengthens us; however, there are some areas in our lives, or rather gifts, that only you can do best. It is imperative that when you set out to do something, that you understand that you can't do five things at the same time. Some tasks require undivided attention, especially in the beginning stage of a project. It is important to have a mission statement for your vision or project, as well as your personal life. Wikipedia defines a mission statement as "a statement of purpose of a company, organization, or person; its reason for existing; a written declaration of an organization's core purpose and focus that normally remains unchanged over time." Know what you stand for.

I have a mission statement for my own life, a reason for my existence. It is a scripture I received from God some years ago. This was right after my first intense fast. I am not suggesting that it is the only way to your mission statement; however, I went seeking and that is what God showed me. When you define your mission statement, it is a guide that always reminds you of what you are doing and why you are doing it. A mission statement can be measurable and requires you to constantly review your progress. This could be your compass to stay on track toward your goals in your business, ministry, and life.

Highlighting my mission statement has been my go-to whenever I forget or feel overwhelmed on my journey.

God has already put in us what we are supposed to be doing and what we are capable off. He knew us before we were formed, and as we grow in him, he slowly reveals to us what we are here for and how we can fulfill our purpose.

The key thing is we must seek after him and build a strong relationship in order to grow in him. We need to be transformed by the renewing of our minds in order to adjust to heavenly wisdom. The Bible says my people perish for lack of knowledge. How many times does it hurt when we have to say "If only I knew"?

I used to be closed-minded; I used to restrict my knowledge to only things that were in line with my belief system and discard those I believed were not.

My pastor taught us to be well-rounded, so that interacting with different people from different walks of life would be easier. Knowledge is key, and you can never accumulate too much of it. Yes, you can have knowledge, but one must decipher what you live by.

"Eyes has not seen, nor ears heard, nor have entered into the heart of man the things which God has prepared for those who love him" (1 Corinthians 2:9, NKJV)

I love this promise because it goes to show that my mind is not big enough to comprehend what he has in store for me. My current dreams are just little nuggets that he has revealed to me because he says—I rephrase—*"Call unto me and I will show you great and mighty things" (See Jeremiah 33:3).* What God can do for me and through me is beyond what my mind can contain currently. It has not entered my heart yet in order for it to be processed by my mind.

It's baffling to me that it's only when my heart receives will my mind be able to translate into words. In other words, God's intent and plan for my life has not even gotten to a place in me where I can begin to decode. It has not entered my heart yet. No wonder his ways are higher than ours, his ways are not our ways. It's also comforting to know that am more than capable of my now. It's exciting to know that if I walk with Him and lean on him for everything, my life will be elevated to a whole new meaning.

I have a short exercise for you and would like you to answer these questions as honestly as possible. This is between you and God, so there's no need to be uncomfortable, secretive, or too spiritual about your answers. It is my hope that after you see this in writing, that is helps to lead you in the right direction.

Are you living your dream life?

Are you working your dream Job?

Are you married to your dream imperfect-perfect partner?

Are you happy where you are in life right now?

Have you been fruitful with what God has entrusted in your hands, and can you pass it on to your children and children's children?

If you could change anything about your current situation, what could it be?

If money was not an issue, what would you do?

Let me break down some of these questions to help you think deeper.

Are you living your dream life?

For most people, the answer to this would be no. Well I hope you can still dream. God already told us that old men shall dream dreams, which lets me know it's never too late to put a plan in action, and it's never too late to start pursuing your dream. You are never too old to dream, you are never too young to start. Once you know, or once you imagine what your dream life should look like, if you never do anything else, at least have a thought in motion that will help trigger ways to keep that dream alive. Allow it to manifest at some point in your life time.

My dad always tells me he has lived a full circle, and his wish for us, his children, is that we do the same and much more.

We all have different capacities of imagination, please be assured that living your dream life is attainable.

Are you working your dream job?

This one is crucial and of all the questions is my favorite. I personally find it fulfilling to be paid for something I enjoy doing— what I refer to as getting paid for my talent. Each one of us has a vision of what our dream job looks like. Mine is to work for me and become an employer. Right now, I'm working for someone, and as much as "I work unto the Lord," I long for my dream. Today, we have dreams and talents at waste because people are afraid of letting go of that salaried job, those benefits, that office, status—the list is endless. It is not easy to stop working and chase after your dream when in one hand, you have a job that guarantees you a dollar amount every week, semi-weekly, or monthly.

I would not highly recommend anyone to stop working if they are not fully persuaded that they are ready to pursue their gift/talent as a source of income. The best part about making money using your gift or talent is that you love it and it takes very little effort to motivate you to do it.

Are you married to your dream imperfect-perfect partner?

Whether or not you are married to your dream spouse, like every dream, it's totally dependent on you. If you are already married, you can always make the best with who you have, and if you are not married, you have an opportunity to put in your request. The Lord Almighty has never failed anyone, and he won't start with you. I wish I could go into more detail about this, but you get the idea.

Are you satisfied with where you are right now?

Yes, not that you can't go any further, and no, simply because you know that you can always do better. Most people are not satisfied with where they are right now anyway. I come with the good news of "Change is on the way." However, the biggest facilitator to the long-awaited change is your next step.

Now that you have answered the questions, whichever one resonates with you the most, write down your strategy on how you're going to change it or make it better. And if you don't know right now, it's okay. Pray that God helps you in that area. Pray he reveals to you what kind of shift you need to be making in your life to see better, work better, do better, and make that change for the better. This includes your spiritual walk, your relationship with God, relationships with others, and your calling.

Many of us fail because of lack of patience. And even though we are pursuing our God-given idea, it doesn't mean it will come together in one day. One idea can give birth to many ideas—it doesn't mean you have to implement them all at the same time.

It's almost fair to assume that having too many responsibilities at a time causes divided attention. One thing may take more time than the other, but when you focus on one thing, it has all your undivided attention increasing probability of success. Being successful is the ultimate goal. In this case, success may simply mean that you complete the work that you committed to. You got the results that were intended for the project. And even though you did a project out of obedience to the voice of God and had no idea the outcome, when you see the fruits of your labor, you know you were successful.

And if you know that God gifted you to do something, then any setbacks, holdups, interruptions, and interceptions should not stop you from pressing forward.

There comes a point in your life as a child of God you realize that you have access and power to so many things, including anything. Jesus once assured us that we shall do greater works.

"[V]erily, verily, I say unto you, he that believeth on me, the works that I do shall he do also; and greater works than these shall he do; because I go unto my father" (John 14:12, NKJV).

This lets me know that we have such a great potential to do whatsoever we desire. We have been given that right through Jesus Christ. When I think about my life and the different industries I have familiarized myself through employment, it lets me know how capable I am of doing anything. Having a degree in one subject does not limit you to one industry. However, you can't study finance and apply to be a physician—"Houston, we have a problem!" And even though we are affiliated with the greatest physician ever known to mankind, there is no way the world is going to hire you as a physician unless you apply as an intercessor or miracle worker.

As much as we are aware that we can do anything, in this case, you can enroll into the medical field and become a physician. It's never too late, and it is not impossible. After all, we have the potential to do it all.

Coming back to the scripture, I know that sometimes, one may find it difficult to relate the scripture to their current life situation; we tune into kingdom work and fail to balance life, our desires, and the will of God. There is nothing wrong with desiring and pursuing a lavish lifestyle as long as it doesn't consume you. Things are to be used and people are to be loved, not the other way around. I believe anything in its natural form is good unless used for bad. A knife is an extraordinary tool used regularly in the household until someone decides it's a murder weapon, then we have something bad to say about the knife. In the same manner, we can pursue the things we want in life. We just have to be cautious of who we can become once we get them.

Plan, Plan, Plan or You Will Fail (Luke 14:28)

5

PLANNING IS SUCH A CRUCIAL stage in facilitating the flow of your project. There is a culture that encourages us to live in the moment and take one day at a time. That may be good in some cases but is not always the smartest thing to do.

God is a God of order, and if we didn't have to plan anything, I am almost certain life would be chaotic.

Part of the reason why planning is important is so that we can be close to perfect in fulfilling our intent.

In order to start something, whether it's a business, project, sport, etc., there is usually planning that takes place, and this may be in the form of research, practice, a business plan and/or studying.

Before I opened my business, I did some research. It was an extremely challenging time for me, I almost gave up.

In the research and planning stage, you may face a lot of opposition and negativity, and it can be very discouraging. You would think the planning stage was challenging, but boy, did it get even more chaotic when I opened the actual business. Some curveballs I was prepared for, and some not at all. As a believer, it's always comforting to know that as long as God is on your side, you will surely find a way. With God, you will always prevail.

Planning helps with keeping your thoughts in line, helping you articulate what it is you are doing. It helps you see the vision better, and when times get tough, the things you have written in order will help you reflect on your mission statement.

It is always important to write your plan out even when you don't know what obstacles you might run into. "You learn as you go." This will allow you to tweak your original plan as needed. Also be prepared to change things around until you can find the perfect course of action for your project. Don't be discouraged if this means continuously evolving or even alternating from one idea to another, then be it.

I found that planning helped me in decision-making, and having to write down my plans helped me see where I was coming from and anticipate where I was going.

When I decided to write this book, I had a goal. My goal was to have the book completed by December 15, 2015 and published by 2016. Having set up this timeline pushed me to set a specific time to write. It was a lot of pressure, and even though things didn't go as planned, the point is, I stayed the course.

I dedicated a specific time daily, and even though I somewhat knew it would be a challenge for me to write at the same time daily, I planned on it as a commitment to my project.

Planning helps put things into perspective, gives value to what you are doing, and helps you develop some level of discipline. It helps you measure progress and success.

Fast forward, 2016 came, and my book was still not finished. Earlier I mentioned that things may change, and you must adjust to the changes as they come. One of the things I realized in "my writing time" was that I sometimes had nothing to write. I guess this is what they call writer's block. Most importantly I realized I was writing by divine inspiration. It wasn't so much about getting it done at a certain period of time, but it was more about translating what God was giving me into words.

I quickly realized that I made the plan, but God was going to order the steps in which the plan would be executed.

"*We can make our plans, but the Lord determines our steps*" (Proverbs 16:9, NLT).

This does not mean my plan was unnecessary. I was able to stay the course because I had a plan. Changes will take place, directions will be switched, and instructions will vary—it's all part of the process. When all this occurs, there is not a problem at all until you make the decision to give up.

In my experience of writing this book, there were times when days would go by, and I had nothing to write, which according to my observation was interfering with completion of my book.

Finally, I had to take note that I was not writing up a manual. It wasn't like I was writing a book with instructions on how to ride a bicycle or how to drive a car. I'm pretty sure that would be an "easier write" because it's a step-by-step structure. In my case, I was writing according to spiritual inspiration, and sometimes, I had to wait longer days in order to receive something to write. I am ecstatic about the fact that someone will read my book one day. It is my sincere hope that someone's life will be blessed and changed forever.

As you become more aware of your vision, ponder on it, and God will pour more and more into you.

After opening myself to a business idea that almost seemed impossibly feasible, my mind suddenly started tapping into seemingly difficult ideas. I had developed a confidence one notch higher than before; I knew what I had been through and anticipated what I was going to go through.

One day, as I was sitting in my quiet time, the Lord brought to my attention that all the wealth that is available to me is in my hands. This is my story. I had decided to customize picture frame messages for my married friends as wedding gifts. In the past, I had painted and crafted similar pieces, pieces of which I didn't particularly think highly of. I dismissed my ability and decided I wanted someone professional to make them for me. When I asked someone professional to make them for me, they let me know they had discontinued customizing. I was frustrated, but later I tapped into my own mind, opened the book of remembrance, and realized I had done this sort of thing before. So I decided to do it myself. I have not nurtured this project as a source of income yet, but it's definitely on the list. I have already gotten in touch with the right people, but like I said, one thing at a time.

Another thing that happened is, I've been told, the little donut snacks I make are delicious. I have a friend who kept on pestering me to start making them in a commercial kitchen for sale. Whenever she brought it to my attention, I would laugh it off. Finally I went to visit friends who own coffee shops and I asked them if I could supply them and they agreed. I have not aggressively pursued that either.

The picture I am painting here is you won't know until you try, and just because an idea sounds ridiculous doesn't mean you can't execute it.

Planning is as good as a starting point. For instance, if you are in college studying to be a medical doctor, you study the courses specific to what kind of a doctor you want to become. If you are a preacher about to hit the pulpit, you prepare through prayer and fasting, or at least I hope you consult with God. And if you are about to be married, you plan for a wedding and prepare for a marriage. The reason we plan/prepare is to be successful in our endeavors.

Not only does planning make your workflow easy, it allows you to measure progress, and it keeps you organized. Now I know some people would still argue that "don't worry about tomorrow because tomorrow will take care of itself." May I remind you that what you do today will determine your tomorrow? The magnitude of your input today has a great impact on the altitude of your outcome tomorrow. And whether or not you pay attention to what your investment is today, you will still reap what you sow.

You will also quickly realize that in order to plan you need to develop a plan for your plan. Make sure is it attainable. Do not set goals you know will be challenging for you. Start simple, and as you master your first attempt, then make changes and challenge yourself with more. Your best is yet to come.

Be Committed

6

COMMITMENT WILL GET YOU RESULTS. One of my favorite quotes is "Discipline and not desire will get you results." When I set out to write this book, one of the things I was worried about was commitment. I knew I wanted to write the book, I told myself I was committed to writing, and I knew I would accomplish my goal. What I was more concerned about was the commitment to the times I had set aside every week to do the writing. On a scale of one to ten, I was at a ten to getting the book done, but the accuracy of being on my computer at the times I set aside was unreliable due to my unfixed schedule. The good news is I planned for it, and I did my best to make it happen. I share this as a result of learning that commitment opens a side of you that teaches you discipline.

I learned that if you don't commit to something/someone, you are likely to be negligent, and when there is neglect, nothing gets done, and when it is not done, then it's a project incomplete; it's a goal unaccomplished, and it can translate into failure.

When a man marries a woman, he is saying that he's committing to her and all that comes with her. He is obliged to give her attention, time, and love and everything else that comes with being in a marriage. Key thing to commitment is time. Whatever you are committed to you find time to do, whether it's work, sports, studies, classes, gym, kids—the list is endless—make it count. Time wasted is never gained. Every second that goes by is a second none of us will ever count again. Time waits for no one. Use it wisely.

It can be demanding to keep up with the never-ending surprises of the day. It's a fight to be on task. You fight to stay committed. And yes things do come up, just stay committed to your commitment.

One thing I can attest to about commitment is the level of ful-fillment that comes with accomplishment. The spirit of a conqueror is manifested, and it surely encourages me to believe that more can be done. In a way, it is a declaration to the Lord that you can be trusted to complete an assignment.

God is committed to us and that won't be changing anytime soon. That makes him God and that gives us assurance of infinite love and protection. I am hopeful that we can apply a similar type of commitment to what God wants to accomplish in us and through us.

Setting a goal is a step towards commitment. By all means pos-sible, try to meet that goal. For instance, if you decide to work out two hours a day at a specific time of the day, do everything in your power to meet that. As time goes by it may change to, two hours at any time of the day. The most important thing remains that you are still committed to some two hours of the twenty-four hours.

I know a lot of people who start but don't finish, and with some projects, I am one of those people. Two things come to mind, lack of motivation and sometimes you ran into a speed bump.

Some bumps we can recover from quicker than a hurry, and some not so fast. Commitment means that no matter what hap-pens, you will complete your assignment. It may take you longer than anticipated, but the main goal is to complete. Commitment can be frustrating. You might want to throw in the towel—this is com-pletely normal. When this happens, look back and think on why you started in the first place. That in itself is ammunition enough for you to keep going. Take time to do something that gets you back in the mood. This could be your kids, your spouse, your vision board, your mama, your surroundings—I am sure you know who/what keeps you pumped.

Another thing to be mindful off is, as you progress, it can become frustrating, discouraging, and challenging. My "go-to" when this happens is to imagine the joy at the end of my journey.

If you are the type of person who has commitment issues, you start but never finish, please get yourself together. I bet you thought I was going to say something different ha-ha-ha. No! Get yourself in order!

Sometimes you are just that person who gets excited about something new and then realize you are not that passionate about it. Try to put your energy to good use.

For those of us who reverence God, we may have trouble committing to our own goals, but when convinced that God instructed us to do something, we can get highly motivated. If it takes you the fear of God to get it done, then be it. Whatever makes it possible use it. There are individuals who are driven by results. These are determined to see results and are committed to exactly that. We all come from different walks of life. One thing we have in common is faith. Some call it determination, overcoming, conquering, perseverance, achieving goals, being successful at the end of the day—all these things require faith and the works to attain results.

Share your vision and goals with someone who cares who matters and/or who benefits.

Stay in the posture of being taught and trained. Start the process today. That vision you have been pushing back needs to be in motion. Start that business, I promise you the money will come.

Reflect

7

As you progress in your ministry, business, sports, goals, or whatever project you are pursing, reflect on where you started. See how the hand of God has moved you from point A to the point you are at now. Every day is an opportunity for you to get to the next point. The limit is endless, and as good as you already are, there's room to get better and enough grace to become great.

When you think about the goodness of the Lord and where he has brought you from, it should encourage you to know that greater is ahead, for he promised us he will bring us to that expected end.

"[F]or I know the thoughts that I think toward you, saith the Lord, thoughts of peace, and not evil, to give you an expected end" (Jeremiah 29:11, NKJV).

This is good enough of a petition to bring before the presence of God. You should be expectant for the manifestation of the promise. One of my favorite scriptures to reflect on is 1 Corinthians 2:9. *"But as it is written, Eye hath not seen, nor ear heard, neither have entered into the heart of man, the things which God hath prepared for them that love him."*

Once again, that scripture. I love how it reminds me that everything I know, love, and hear about God is nothing compared to what he has prepared for me. My mind cannot begin to fathom or even guess what His capable of. No eye has seen it yet, no ear has heard, and no heart is beating hard enough to harbor what the Lord has prepared for us. It has not yet entered the hearts of men, and only God knows what is in one's heart, meaning if something is in my heart, it is unknown to me and to all mankind until there's a manifestation. Better yet, it has not entered any heart of man. This suggests that you will never fully grasp the altitude of what God can and will do for you. But if you let him, you will surely test and see that he is all powerful.

When David had to tell Saul that he could take up Goliath, he reflected. He talked about how he overcame the bear and the lion.

> *And David said unto Saul, They Servant kept his father's sheep, and there came a lion, and a bear, and took a lamb out of the flock:*
> *And I went out after him, and smote him, and delivered it out of his mouth: and when he arose against me, I caught him by his beard, and smote him, and slew him.* (1 Samuel 17:34–35, NKJV)

David's confidence is clearly coming from experience. In the same manner, we also can reflect on our past victories and conclude that "if he did it before, then he can do it again."

Nothing is new under the sun. Not even the challenges that seem new to us.

Whatever we face in life, we can trace it back to the same God who is triumphant in victory. He is mighty in battle and remains to this day, the matchless, eternal undefeated one. He created everything and nothing can defeat its creator.

When you reflect on your many past victories, trust and believe there's more to come. He did it the first, the second, and the last time, and he will continue doing it. He is just that perfect.

Many times, I've found myself in similar or identical trials, and I am reminded that I got out. I don't always remember how I got out; however, one thing is for sure: I am not in the same predicament. His methods pleasantly surprise me.

Being able to reflect is supposed to trigger an attitude of gratitude. If you can look back and see that you are not the same person you used to be, for every challenge you faced, he rescued you, and you have accomplished and made progress in life, you ought to be thankful.

Growing up, most of us can recall when our parents would tell us to say "thank you" for every time something was done for us. I believe it works the same with God. I am convinced that he will do more, the more we appreciate. I also believe a thankful attitude makes you dwell less on the negative side of things.

Thank him for what you have, what he has done, what he is doing, and what he is about to do. Use your past victories as a reminder of the victories to come.

God is forever pouring out his blessings. At times we get so caught up on a specific need that we overlook what has already been given to us. And for some of us, we are already onto the next without taking the time to grasp the current blessing.

God blesses us in mysterious and numerous ways. We need not to forget that whatever situation or need we have, he is able to do much more than we can think ask or even imagine.

Don't limit your expectations from God. Just because it doesn't happen in the same way it did last time does not mean it won't happen. In the moment of anticipation, time becomes your enemy. Patience can be a real challenge. If you wait just a little while longer, it will be worth the wait.

One of the reasons it was so important for me to maintain an attitude of gratitude was that I felt I wasn't thankful enough. I found myself testifying today and complaining the next. I had to overcome that feeling by giving more. Anything I give now is symbolic to me, simply because you never know what door opens for you through the act of giving. "I have because I give." "I don't give because I have."

I happened to go through a time period where it felt like my victories seemed to be short-lived. It felt like before I could finish celebrating one thing, something negative came up and overshadowed my victory. And sometimes my victory turned into misery. When God is pushing you into greatness, he moves anything and anyone that needs to go out of the way, and he brings in what/who you need.

The reason we sometimes feel our victories are short-lived is because we are probably in the wrong position. Sometimes we chase after a temporal thing. It won't last because you need to keep pressing forward, so you can find your right position. And even after you find that position, be prepared to move again when it's time to move. There is no need to get comfortable you need to keep it pushing. Students have courses, classes, phases, grades, etc. Every first grader must be prepared to go to the second grade. We must apply the same concept. And when fear creeps in as you are about to move to the next level, reflect on the many years that have gone by and think on how he has sustained you. God's resume is incomparable to no other. It is perfect! His track record is nothing that we will ever understand. Trust him because his surprises are endless. He is a matchless king, the beginning yet the end, a man yet fully God, a shepherd yet a priest, a lamb yet a lion, and he is one but three, the chief cornerstone yet the rock of ages. Who but God has such credentials? The more I think of his various forms and the many forms he has manifested in my life, I can't help but serve him and honor him with my life.

The greatness and might of God sometimes makes me wonder why he associates with us. Just like the angels wonder, *What is man that you are so mindful of him?*

I am reminded of how important I am to God, and I know for a fact that he intentionally created me.

God is always thinking about you and me and is consistently mindful of our endeavors. All we have to do is let him lead.

Don't Worry about the How, Be More Concerned about the When

―――――――――― ∿∽⟋⟍⟋⟍⟋⟍∽∿ ――――――――――

8

IT SEEMINGLY BECOMES DIFFICULT TO envision the when and how, and if not left for God, this can be discouraging. Sometimes you wonder, *How are things going to turn out given my current circumstances?* I find it easier to envision what the result would feel or look like when I finally see the final product. You will find that engaging in the imagination of the outcome can be the push it takes.

I love the quote, "If your mind can conceive it, then you can have it." Whatever your mind sees or creates, know that it can be attained. This works both ways positive and negative. You chose which way you want it to work for you. This is something you may need to practice when you begin to worry about the whens and the hows.

The bible says as a man thinketh so is he. Whatever you entertain in your mind you become.

"*[F]or as he thinketh in his heart, so is he*" (Proverbs 23:7, NKJV).

The mind is at liberty of exploring all kinds of thoughts, and our thoughts become our words and eventually the manifestation of things spoken into being.

I have already addressed the topic of the tongue and its power. Speaking positively into your own life brings forth results. Speak it into existence. Tame your thoughts and make sure your mind is filled with more positive things. Bad, evil, and negative thoughts can derail good things to come.

As you practice speaking the good into existence, some things will manifest almost immediately, and some will take time. Do not be discouraged most good things take time. Some foundations take longer to build than others. Imagining the thing that you want to come into being and possessing it will help give you a good feeling and keep you focused on the prize.

Thinking about the how can also be frightening because the pressure involved in putting the pieces together especially when we can't trace the pieces can be too much to handle.

When I decided to start my business, I was so invested in getting it started that I didn't worry about the "how." I knew money was the biggest part of it. Research, marketing, and a lot more would be needed, but most importantly I was determined to start. One of the biggest and hardest buttons to press is the start button. A lot of us have great ideas that are millions of dollars' generators, but we just don't have the guts to translate the ideas into tangible goods. If you are serious, start by simply making Google and YouTube your best friend. Check in with them and see what they know about your subject of interest. Then start.

In business, I learned that money is not the biggest challenge, but that you must be generating ideas constantly. I found that having money only to execute was not enough. I learned that creating ideas would generate that cash flow I was looking for. Therefore, innovation is important. One idea can become a lot of people's idea, and differentiation and innovation will help boost and bring forth more business and income with ideas that stand out. In each one of us is creative power. Your wealth is on the inside of you, get wisdom, and favor will come upon you. God will open doors that man can't shut. Always remember that we walk by faith and not by sight. One way to know your faith is at work is when you press forward and are worry-free.

It's not always what it looks like. And this goes either side. Sometimes something/someone looks good or feels good, and it turns out to be the wrong choice. And other times something/someone may not seem like the right choice, and it turns out to be the best decision you have ever made. Be open to trying and learning new things daily.

Be Fruitful and Multiply

9

THIS REMINDS ME OF THE men who were given talents in the twenty-fifth chapter of the book of Mathew starting from verse 15. We see in this passage that the man who was entrusted with five talents traded for five more and the one with two gained two more and the one with the one talent hid it and had nothing to show for when it was time to review.

And unto one he gave five talents, to another two, and to another one; to every man according to his several ability; and straightway took his journey. Then he that had received the five talents went and traded with the same, and made them other five talents. And likewise he that had received two, he also gained other two. But he that had received one went and digged in the earth, and hid his lord's money. After a long time the lord of those servants cometh, and reckoneth with them. And so he that had received five talents came and brought other five talents, saying, Lord, thou deliveredst unto me five talents: behold, I have gained beside them five talents more. His lord said unto him, Well done, thou good and faithful servant: thou hast been faithful over a few things, I will make thee ruler over many things: enter thou into the joy of thy lord. He also that had received two talents came and said, Lord, thou deliveredst unto me two talents: behold, I have gained two other talents beside them. His lord said unto him, Well done, good and faithful servant; thou hast been faithful over a few things, I will make thee ruler over many things: enter thou into the joy of thy lord. Then he which had received the one talent came and said, Lord, I knew thee that thou art an hard man, reaping where thou hast not sown, and gathering where thou hast not strawed: And I was afraid, and went and hid thy talent in the earth: lo, there thou hast that is thine. His lord answered and said unto him, Thou wicked and slothful servant, thou knewest that I reap where I sowed not, and gather where I have not strawed: Thou oughtest therefore to have put my money to the exchangers, and then at my coming I should have received mine own with usury. Take therefore the talent from him, and give it unto him which hath ten talents. For unto every one that hath shall be given, and he shall have abundance: but from him that hath not shall be taken away even that which he hath. (Mathew 25:15–29, NKJV)

I want to point out a few things here. It says something about the man who was entrusted with five talents. His character was trustworthy for the Lord to give him five talents because the Lord knows best. I believe it's safe to say God Almighty knows what kind of stewards we are; he will entrust us with his gifts according to our capabilities. I can also say the one with the two talents is steadily working his way up to be entrusted with more. Once proven capable, more is given. And the man with the one talent, unfortunately he had proven not to be a good steward and ended up losing the one talent he had.

God has already given us wealth through the gifts he has given us. These gifts we already possess in us, there is no need to ask for them. Our full-time duty is to discover them, use them, and empower others to do the same, and that's how we multiply. Once again, these gifts can be used as a source of income as well as a support system for the many assignments God has given us.

What you need to break forth in business is to cultivate your talent into a product/service that will generate you income. Be fruitful and multiply. You wonder, *How can I break forth in my music when everyone is singing?* That's a reasonable question; however, there is no other person in this world that sings like you do. There is not another person in this world that plays an instrument like you do. They may seem to sing or play better than you, but remember they are not you. Only you have the power to do it the way you do. Share with the rest of the world why you are different. In the kingdom of God, there is no competition. We are all uniquely created, and I personally measure this by admiring one's ability to exercise their talent.

However, companies/businesses that are successful and well-established have already put a mark on their consumers. From there, they tweak, compliment, and improve the same product to get more sales. In business, there is competition.

To apply this to our lives, we must be willing to evolve in order to make a difference. Even God doesn't like you sitting in the same position doing the same thing over and over. On your current job, I hope you are looking forward to a promotion or early retirement. If you are in school, make your grades better. Improve your skills in whatever you are doing. Desire to do better and become better at anything and everything you are currently doing.

I personally try to apply this technique across the board spiritually, emotionally, socially, physically, and mentally. One of the things I watch very closely is my spiritual growth, and one thing I have noticed is that every either end of the year or beginning of a new year, I speak in different tongues. It's not something I consciously monitored, but when I was into my third year of new tongues, I noticed it. This time not only did I get new tongues, but God graced me with the gift of faith, something I had been longing for, for a long time. The point I am trying to make is, whatever you have now can grow. You can multiply it. Whether it's your faith, your money, your prayer life, the point is it can grow, and you can increase on every side.

As we increase, let us remember why. God blesses us so we can be a blessing unto others. As fruitful as God makes you, be sure to multiply. While you are able to bear fruit, whatever fruit may represent in your life, think of ways to multiply and give to others. The gifts that God has given us are meant to be utilized.

If the gifts are not used, they become dormant, and then they seem to be nonexistent. And it's not that they're nonexistent, it's that they're are neglected. The gifts of the Lord are without repentance meaning that once God has given you a gift, he does not turn around and take it back. If you don't use it, then it's just as good as not having it.

Now it's one thing having the gift, and it's another having the anointing of God on your life. Gifts have been given to all of us, but the anointing of God is given to a selected group. All good things come from God, and every good and perfect gift is from God. Since the gift is from God, it means we have the ability to do well and be excellent at this gift.

I believe to be able to exercise this gift back to the glory of God requires anointing. Not everyone is using their gifts to glorify God. Some people use their gifts to edify themselves and glorify the devil by causing others to stumble.

I believe we all have gifts and the difference is that some people use them, and some people don't. Unfortunately, so many gifts are going to waste.

When you discover something in you that's able to generate income or something of value, stick to it and learn more ways to make more of it. This can be anything from helping others, giving of your time, healing, and encouraging others, or giving of your money. The point is to use what is already in you.

Try not to become complacent even in your well-doing, especially in your walk with God. You cannot spend less time with God and think that you will grow. You need to spend more time with him; get into the Word of God, study it until it becomes a part of your life. Allow yourself to grow in the Word until it becomes the guideline you live by. Absorb as much as you can till you overflow. Even reading the Word by itself is never enough. One needs to study the Word and engage into further research. Make use of the concordance, read the Strong's, look back into history, and look into what the theologians have discovered. This will help you increase your knowledge and understanding of the Word.

In the same manner, in order to be fruitful and to multiply what you already have, you need to strategize and strive for more. You need to expand in that area of interest.

What do you do when you have so many ideas but are missing the courage to execute? Keep in mind that an idea is considered as a step on it's on.

Nowadays we have Google and YouTube. The two will answer almost any question you have. There are some nonprofit organizations that will help you with your business plan. And yes, challenging times will come. Trust me, it's doable. You will definitely need more than a valium to stay committed and to maintain your cool during this journey. The main thing is that you continue moving.

In anything you do, the idea is that you become better, produce more, and sell more. We can agree to some level that more is good. Aim high on your job for a promotion or a raise. In business, you work to better the business, increase clients which translates into increased sales, more employees, which mostly translates into a successful business. I would hope that whatever you do, you do it for the greater good. And even if it's voluntary work, do it to make a positive difference.

He Is Pushing You and Pulling You

10

As HARD AS THE GOING may seem, trust and believe God is pulling and pushing you at the same time. He is your advocate throughout the process. It's not a foreign concept that at some point you will get complacent. After working so hard for so long, sometimes you pause to enjoy that stress free window. Be cautious not to become too comfortable.

For some people, reflecting on how challenging the journey was is the push or pull that drives them to continue.

I remember feeling at ease after the sleepless nights and the long stressful days of building my business. I came to a point where the picture was becoming clearer.

However, I knew I still needed to do more. For weeks, I had been thinking about how hard it can get to want more. More meant more tears, more time, more money, more stress, etc. I feared to embrace more because I just couldn't get past what I had been through. I would think about "more," then turn around, and scare myself out of it.

"[W]hen someone has been given much, much will be required in return, when someone has been entrusted with much, even much more will be required" (Luke 12:48, NLT).

Finally, one evening, I decide/thought was ready for more. I was aware there was a cost to more, I just had no clue the price. Here goes! My decision is final "I want more." As Sunday morning approached, I was hot and ready and comfortable with my decision. I get to church that morning only to have my pastor's wife confirm my decision through the preaching of the word. At this point, I am nervous at how things are unfolding but confident. Little did I know it would cost me more than I imagined. The point I am trying to make here is, there is always a cost to get to the next level, but it should not stop you.

When God wants you to move to the next level, he pushes you and pulls you toward that direction. For instance, I kept on hearing about my next level in one form or another. I kept crossing paths with my push through sermons, the Bible, random conversations, media, and I recognized God pushing and pulling me both at the same time. When I finally decided to act upon my push, it costed me my entire business and everything I knew how to do at the time. My business world as I knew it crumbled right before my eyes.

I didn't immediately recognize that it was a response to my next level request. It just seemed like a nightmare I needed to awaken from. You can never anticipate the cost of the "next level," but fear not for he is your push and your pull.

The saying "What doesn't kill you makes you stronger" is not too far off. Some trials can be mind-blowing, it almost feels like you can never recover from them. Likewise, when you look back to some of the challenges, you can't remember the details of the trauma. Everything we go through today has a role to play in tomorrow. At times it's unclear and may seem too much to bear, but the Lord knows it all.

> "My thoughts are nothing like your thoughts," says the Lord. "And my ways are far beyond anything you could imagine. For just as the heavens are higher than the earth, so my ways are higher than your ways and my thoughts higher than your thoughts." (Isaiah 55:8–9, NLT)

If you knew how God would work out every detail of your life, then he ceases to be God. God is that awesome.

It's easy to want things to change or play out the way you would prefer. I get it, it can be frustrating to wait on God. The only and best option is to wait. And if you are as impatient as I am, you might have to repeat some lessons over and over.

In some of my experiences when I get extremely impatient/frustrated, it's usually when am the closest to my blessing.

God always knows how to soothe a heart or mind that goes through the moment of "I wonder if he can hear me." The hardest part is the going through, but the best part is that you are just going through, and sooner than later you will be past that stage.

God is your uttermost biggest cheerleader, and no matter what you do, you cannot outdo him. There will be times when your adrenaline rush will tap into places and spaces of your mind that you don't know exist. The power and the spirit of God will push you there. When your push seems to fail you, His mighty hand will be right there to pull you. And when you procrastinate to the pull, sometimes the push can feel a little rough. So whether He pulls you or pushes you, it's all working out for your good—which leaves me no choice but to remind you to recognize his voice, his leading, his guidance, and his instructions.

A perfect example of recognizing his "push" or "pull" is when you find yourself revisiting an idea that won't go away no matter how hard you try to ignore it or shake it off. At some point, it will register that the one only way it will go away is by acting on it. And now that you have decided to take action, guess what? He will honor his promise to you throughout your journey. Stay the course. There's more work to be done and visions to be manifested. Through it all, push yourself. Be accountable for your own time. Never stop trying to get better. Whether it's a job, cooking, serving in whichever capacity, give it your best. Doing things with a passion will open doors and get you places you never imagined. You will meet and rub shoulders with people beyond your wildest imagination. Put your passion and gifts to work. Whatever you do, strive for a 110 percent, and if you can do more, even better.

Pray, Pray, then Pray, and then Pray Some More

11

STOP AND PRAY THROUGH THE entire process. Always remember to thank him for the hurdles you have completed, the hurdles you are currently working on, and the ones yet to come. There's a saying that goes, "You are either going through, you just got through, or you are just about to go through." With that in mind, you will need a support system to help you go through the going. The only ultimate strength that will ever exist is the strength of God.

Things come and go, people come and go, but God is the same yesterday, today, and forever. From everlasting to everlasting, he will remain the same.

Permit me to share what prayer has done for me since I discovered it. In the last years through my trials and tribulations, I became acquainted with prayer. I went through some hard times. It seemed like prayer wasn't working for me. It wasn't because I tried it, and it never worked, it was because I looked at God through my problem instead of looking at my problem through God.

I was fully aware that my praise, prayer life, and relationship toward God was independent of my trials, but some trials seemed to overtake me and overshadow God's power—at least I thought.

However, as I drew closer to him through the exercise of prayer, I became more aware of his miraculous hand. I became one of many candidates of his precious miracles. What I've learned about prayer in the many few years I have been around this earth is that there's nothing new under the sun. God has proven himself more times than I can keep track off. I would be foolish not to be believe him. And for every time he proves himself, I feel silly for magnifying the minute challenges I face.

I had to find a way to separate what I was/am going through and who he is to me. I also acknowledged that my life was dependent on prayer as much as it was dependent on his Word, "the Bible."

So then I turned to the question, *Why is it that when I pray, after a while, I get tired or frustrated about praying over the same thing?* For a reason not surprising to many, after a while, I expected an answer. Keep in mind when I say a while, am referring to days, months, sometimes years, and still counting. And periodically you have those deadline trials (you know what I am talking about). If you don't pay by this date, then?

Anyways, I hated feeling that way, so I developed a better relationship with God. *Whether or not you answer me, you are still God, and you will always be worthy of all the praise, the glory, and the honor.* When I got the hang of it, I promise you, no matter the trial when I engage in prayer it is the most amazing time of the day. Don't be fooled I still cry sometimes; however, I am able to push through the pain and past the tears.

The last time I went through a trial that felt like it was going to kill me. The only time I had peace and felt normal was when I was in prayer.

Even though I found myself crying in praise and worship, it was an overwhelming feeling to still be able to connect with him. It was such a soothing feeling I couldn't help but look forward to those moments.

Let me back it up and tell you a little story about how I learned to pray. Once upon a time I was curious about prayer and fasting. At the time, TBN was my main source of biblical knowledge. One day when I was watching TBN, someone on TV was talking about how they prayed for extended hours. I thought to myself, *I wonder what that is like?* I was on a six-to-six fast at the time, so I decided I would pray throughout the last six hours of my fast. I engaged in prayer in what felt like a very long time only to say, "Amen," and it was only forty-five minutes. I was disappointed but grateful that I tried.

The next day, I went to church, and there was a visitor at the church giving her testimony. In her testimony, she mentioned she used to drive three hours to attend a church for overnight prayer. Immediately my eyes lit up, thinking, *Ah-ha! This is who I should be talking to*. I met with her after church service. We connected very quickly as we shared so much in common. I expressed my love and interest in this new lifestyle called fasting and prayer.

In our conversation, she invited me to visit her on a Friday so we could pray all night. I looked forward to Friday. I talked about it all week, and the excitement was clear I was seeking for God. My soul was searching, and anywhere I could find him I was ready to go.

Friday came around, and I had a list of 111 topics to pray about.

I had assumed the night was so long. I remember having prayer topics of things I wanted God to do for me. When I had exhausted that list, I proceeded to put my friends' needs and then added names of people in my sphere of influence that I knew had not accepted Christ as their personal savior. I felt prepared for the prayer meeting. I presented this to her. She smiled and said nothing.

We started praying around 10:00 p.m. This included praise and worship, reading of the Word, short discussions, and prayer.

Let's just say, I now have a better understanding when someone says, "The night is young." Before I knew it, it was 6:47 a.m. My list was nowhere close to being done. God took over the meeting. It was spirit led and not as Charlotte thought. I learned a very important lesson that day. I learned how to flow in the direction of the Holy Spirit.

The next day, I called all my friends and told them about the amazing experience I had. I suggested we make Friday night our prayer night, and to my surprise, everyone was excited about it and willing to be a part of it as well.

Next Friday came, and this time, instead of the two, there were ten of us. Oh yes, ten of us! Some friends had come from surrounding cities as well. God moved his weight, and we had yet another spirit-filled night. The following Friday, only four of us showed up. The number of participants fluctuated, but our excitement did not. Our venues also changed until I asked my pastor at the time, Pastor Jacqueline Theresa Thomas, if we could use the church, and she said yes. Long story short, we named the group Gatekeepers. At this point, God had defined the group. Since we all were members of different churches, each one of us was a watchman for the church they belonged to. Together, we were the watchmen for the city of Pocatello. Gatekeepers continued meeting every Friday night at Praise Temple of God in Pocatello, Idaho for more than eight years and counting.

When Gatekeepers was first started, I had a different agenda for our meetings. Later, I realized God was working out his agenda. He led people to the group, who transformed the group into an international ministry. It reminds me that we sometimes have a small plan, and God has a bigger plan in mind.

Fast forward to the present, prayer has sustained me through all the ups and downs of my life. I would not change that faithful day that helped me learn to navigate the paths of life.

Prayer is such a strong tool, and its strength is undeniable.

I have been through many trials, some highs and lows. Some "lows" didn't last as long as others, while some just seemed to drag on. It always helped to imagine the end of the trial, what it would look like, or how I would feel. This was a way for me to trace my past victories. It's always a good reminder to know that "if he did it before, he can do it again."

When I went through a depression in my life—well, I've been through a few of those episodes. Each episode, I responded differently. During some of these episodes, I masked my feelings by drowning myself with work just so I could refrain from thinking about what I was going through.

The experience that hit me the hardest was when I lost my business to a fire. This was unbearable, and to my surprise, it affected me more than I anticipated. It shocked me that I was confused and failed to understand why I was so hurt. The Charlotte I knew was accustomed to bouncing right back, but this time it was different.

For about a week and a half, I didn't feel or think about the loss of my business. Three weeks later, it hit me like a ton of bricks, and from that point on, it went downhill. I constantly thought of what I could have been doing as this was my full-time job. Not being able to think what my next step would be and having a clouded mind, it became more difficult to function. I isolated myself from the world and wallowed in my pain and misery. Finally, I decided I needed counseling.

My relationship with God is such that I don't only praise and worship him when it's convenient for me; I do so even when I am at a low point.

What I consider my lowest point in my life history, I recall being able to pray, pray, and pray some more. And it was only during prayer time that I felt invigorated. Everything in me seemed chaotic and pointless no matter what I did. Whether I was awake or asleep, the thoughts and the pain seemed endless.

At this time, I found some information about where I could go for counseling. By the time the appointment to meet with the counselor came around, I had already decided I wanted to write a book and start piano lessons to distract myself. I still signed up for counseling and went through a very long intake process. For me, this was an indication that I didn't need this service at this time. I have nothing against counseling. One of the reasons I was interested in talking to someone was so I could hear myself express what I was feeling on the inside. I hoped that I could help me see where I was having the hang up. I wanted to put a name to my feelings. Long story short, I went for the second time, finished my intake, and from then on struggled to follow through.

I felt that a half hour session was not enough for me to unpack my baggage. And when the counselor had asked me to write down my feelings and do a log each day, my facial expression said, "Aaah no, I already budgeted writing time to my book." Yes, my face said all that. In that moment, with all the questions he had asked me during the intake, I came to the conclusion that I did not need a counselor. I already have the best counselor there is in this world. None can be compared to him—not above the earth, not beneath, or in between.

"For unto us a child is born, unto us a son is given, and the government shall be upon his shoulder: and his name shall be called Wonderful, Counsellor, The mighty God, The everlasting Father, The Prince of Peace" (Isaiah 9:6, NKJV).

My desire to do anything or go anywhere was still diminishing, and even though I hated not doing anything, my mind could not jump start. I was unmotivated to look for a job or use my time wisely. One thing I knew was helping me was when I dwelled in the secret place of the most high.

Sundays were not the best of my days out because I had to double up on masking my feelings. I felt compelled to walk around with a smile when in reality, it contradicted my true feelings. I didn't want to be around people's well wishes and apologies for my loss. I was still struggling to make peace with it.

Your loving family and friends can be a trigger, reminding you of "that thing" you are trying to forget. It is a good thing to have people that are concerned about you. And even though I dreaded having to deal with all the questions and concerns of my church family, I pressed my way to church. I did the best I could to harbor my feelings and focus on praising God; after all that's the reason I went to church. I recall Sunday after Sunday, God was consistently encouraging me and reminding me of his promises for me. I would cry hysterically either in service or out of service as I recognized God was clear about his promise for me. At this point, it became blatant that I needed to be in church every Sunday.

Prayer, praise, worship, and fellowship can pull you out of any misery. God's hand is never too short to reach you wherever you are. I know that this is familiar to some people, and for some it's still a struggle to understand or see what God's plan is when times are hard. The good news is God is ready to make it very clear to anyone who seeks to know what his perfect will is in whatever situation you are faced with.

When you read the Bible, you see a good number of individuals that God used in their time of distress. Sometimes that low point is a setup for the better.

Sometimes it's rebuke, but either way, it stands to prove it's for a better reason. My own story tells it. In my low point, I enjoyed my prayer time and longed to be in prayer just a little while longer. It was the only place that felt safe and made sense for me. In a time, such as this I knew that only God would soothe me. Whose strength but God's can get you up, lead you to write a book, and learn to play an instrument as beautiful as the piano? All of this at a time when the world seemed to be against me.

If I didn't have a moment to slow down, even though it was not by choice, I would have never known how serious and passionate I was about the piano. I would have never gotten to share this book with you all. This all happened as a result of what I call a divine interception. The story behind is, I had prayed for God to do what he wanted to do through me to get me to the next level. I firmly expressed I was ready. Two weeks later, my business burned down. The next level is painful and comes at a cost, but it's definitely worth it. The boot camp for the next level in God is definitely not easy nor pleasant; however, graduation, like any other graduation, is a celebration worthwhile for the keys to more opportunities.

Prayer will get you through anything and everything. I am living proof of that. Every now and then I run into people who refer to me as "too spiritual." There's nothing wrong with that.

People will try to reason with you from an ungodly perspective, but when you've lived a life where you understand that without him you are nothing, you can't be swayed. There is enough evidence around me I couldn't be bothered. I'll stay in my lane that guarantees me to my next destination.

Prayer can be a sensitive topic for many. We can all relate to a time we have prayed, and nothing happened or at least we thought. There were times we prayed then threw in the towel. I say it like this, as much and as long as you have prayed, believe it or not, there is a bridge that you have been building. Anytime from today, you will be able to cross over to the other side. This bridge is special with a strong foundation. It has been patiently built with your long time prayers.

The key is that you don't stop. Keep praying for that son, that daughter, that mother/father, that sibling, and loved one. Keep on seeking, asking, and knocking one of these days a door is about to sling open just for you. As they talk about how bad your situation is, keep building that bridge. The best part about crossing over to the other side on a bridge you built is you become officially certified as an engineer of prayer. The ones that laughed at you will announce your certification.

There is no need to be upset with the challenges you face called people. There are not your enemies. The real enemy is out there. Not only is he trying to make you feel frustrated, sad, and angry at the people around you, he wants to do all that and much more. His main goal is to kill steal and destroy. Don't buy into it.

As people talk bad about you or laugh at your circumstance, use that in your petition to pray. I promise you they will be able to retell your story. They will tell it better than you can. They will eat their words. Worry not and keep your eyes on the prize. Yes, I know sometimes it's hard to ignore. I know it can be hard to still love the saints that talk bad about you. Do your best to shake it off lest you delay you on your journey.

We are all embarked on a long journey. It will be wise to take note of the speed limit, cautions, signs, and instructions as we travel. Any missed instructions can cost us more than we think.

I can't emphasize enough about prayer. Prayer has the answers to most if not all the questions you have. On day, when you realize you have taken the wrong turn, prayer will lead you back to the right path. In the case where you do wrong, and it feels like God will never love you again, prayer will bring you back to the place where you can boldly go before the throne of grace and obtain mercy. Prayer is one of the greatest tools we have been given to change and turn lives and situations around. Prayer is one of the greatest tools given to mankind. You can speak things into existence, and they become. Prayer can usher you into the unseen yet the real world. I can't tell it all how much prayer has helped me.

I recall numerous times I felt hopeless, defeated, and good for nothing. Only the power of prayer dug me out of those pits. Through prayer, I have been blessed with a good number of loyal friends. I have friends who pray for me more than I pray for myself. As a young minister of the gospel, it has been challenging knowing that my first duty is to serve him through ministry. It has not been an easy road; however, he chose me, and if he did, it means I have the ability to fulfil the job. Over and over I've asked myself, *When do I put the hat of ministry down?* The more I asked, the more I understood my position in Christ.

I am gracefully embracing it, and as hard as it gets, I no longer ask. I am opening myself to the fact that my hat can only get bigger from this point. All I can do is prepare myself, even though I feel like there is not much preparation you can put into God's surprises. Any man or woman of God understands what I am talking about. It applies to all of us who have acknowledged that Jesus is indeed the Christ, the Lord of lords and King of kings.

Prayer will reveal the secrets of the Bible. The more you engage in it, the more you learn, and the more you learn, the more you realize you don't know. The living Word of God is essential for prayer. Read it, breathe it, eat it. The Word always comes in handy. It keeps you in the right lane, the correct speed limit, and helps you see the cautions and better yet how many miles you have left before you get to your next stop. The Word of God is life. It is meant to be applied to our everyday being. The Bible should not just be a book you read to feel good about yourself and check your list to say you have done your good deed for the day. Your Bible is your navigation system for your life. Try it, and I guarantee you it will not fail you.

I am sold out to prayer because I have more than enough personal experiences and encounters with the power of prayer. I have also had experiences where I prayed for a specific need, got weary in praying about the same topic, and threw in the towel. But our bond is so strong that not praying does me no good. So I quickly snap out of it and get back on the altar. I have been kept calm and patient through prayer.

I am almost certain you can relate to how one can easily become the joke of the house, school, community, or even your church. Our very own dear saints and a'ints can make a mockery of one's longtime "situation." Sometimes it's so bad they tend to identify you by your challenge. Anyone who has experienced what am talking about will testify that it is not a fun thing at all.

Then we have situations where people want to narrate your story. They want to give you a reason or reasons why your situation has not yet changed. They offer their unsolicited opinions. What they forget is every person living today has needs they have been waiting on for a long time, but of course, it is easier to see someone else's when the need is different from yours. Forget not, the scenario is the same we are all waiting for the story to change. It's just that some take longer than others.

Next, we have situations where others are embarrassed on your behalf. They are ashamed of your situation because you have been waiting on God for a very long time (very long time according to whose watch?).

And then you have this one situation, my favorite, where one comes out of their situation and turns right around to look down on people who are still facing their giant. I find this very interesting because I am sure anyone who has been serving the Lord long enough should know that we always go through the cycle of (a) *I am about to go through*, (b) *I am going through*, or (c) *I just came out of it*. I wish it was true that there's no such thing as "going through." It would be much easier for all of us. One thing I've learnt for myself is the *going through* is all part of the process of making you stronger. I believe it's a process that keeps us from being complacent.

Imagine if after overcoming all the challenges you have faced so far, there was a maximum limit. Imagine if there were different categories of challenges, and once you overcome one of each, then you never have to face that "thing" again. Let me break it down for you: what if you have faced the pain of losing a loved one, and it meant you would never have to experience that type of pain again? Meaning you graduate and won't have to face that pain again. Imagine if since you already faced the pain of disappointment, you could check it off your list and never have to worry about disappointment again. Heartbreak/betrayal, then you won't have to go through it again; the loss of something valuable to you perhaps a job, a relationship/marriage, house, and/or a car.

Imagine if life meant that after you've been through any of the things listed, then you wouldn't face any of them again. Wouldn't it be amazing? I know that it would be easier for me because then, I would be looking forward to the last category of pain. After I am done with the last one, I would never have to worry about prayer, fasting, or the energy to evolve in my walk with Christ.

But thank God he didn't design life that way. His intent for us was to achieve everything he has for us. Without facing the pressure, we wouldn't have known what we are capable off. We wouldn't pray ourselves through to the next level in life. The most important thing to remember is that prayer will give you access to your innermost desire. Prayer is the answer to all your questions, and just because nothing has happened after so many years of prayer, don't be discouraged. A time is coming when your story will change. I know it hurts to hear everyone talk about it or talk about you. The truth is you are too significant to be ignored. If you think this is the last time you will be talked about, think again. You are a testimony in your own way, and as bad as it feels to go through your longtime situation, guess what? He chose you to witness in that area. It will all pay off, and the longer you have to wait, the better the results. Be of good courage. God is still alive and has not forgotten your dreams and desires. Keep on praying, and if he fails you, you will be the first in history.

Awaken to the fact that you are engaged in a war. When you are a born-again Christian, you probably already know this, that it's war to keep what you have and its war to get what you want. It's war to love, and it's even a greater war staying in love. It's war to be blessed and an even greater war to stay blessed. The main reason it's war is the enemy is constantly trying to steal from you. He wants to attack you and your blessing. Sometimes he attacks before you can get a hold of your blessing. Suddenly he causes you to wait longer than you wanted to. Tarry just a little while longer on that topic. As interesting as this may seem, we can ask Daniel to see what happened to him

"But the prince of the kingdom of Persia withstood me one and twenty days: but, lo, Michael, one of the chief princes, came to help me; and remained there with the king of Persia" (Daniel 10:13, NKJV).

The Scripture shows another of many possible reasons we face hang-ups. At the end of it all, we see that Daniel persistently prayed until he received. What was already released to him before he could finish praying got to him in twenty-one days. This goes to show you how persistent in prayer we must be. We must keep praying until the answer comes. Anyone who is committed to prayer must have some level of understanding and belief that God will respond. Otherwise why else would you pray? First thing is Daniel prayed, and even though he didn't know that God had already answered, he persisted in prayer. Sounds like God has an immediate answer. When Daniel didn't see the answer immediately, he prayed some more. Finally twenty days later, the answer was fully manifested. Notice that the verse says, *"[W]ith-stood me one and twenty days."* It was interesting to me that it was not summed up as twenty-one days. My take on this is it is significant to acknowledge, the blessing was released on the very first day he prayed. However, not only was it withstood one day but twenty more days.

"And it shall come to pass, that before they call, I will answer; and while they are yet speaking, I will hear" (Isaiah 65:24).

I am trying to encourage someone to understand that he releases before you finish praying. He is very capable of blessing you right away. I and many others are a witness to this.

The Bible encourages us to pray without ceasing. And yes, I know, I am also one of many who have had to pray, pray, and pray some more. The results are always breath taking. Honestly speaking, I've been in situations where I had to pray about a need so much to the extent where I became emotionally detached to my request. Prayer became a natural response. I got so used to praying about the same topic, it became my daily bread ha-ha-ha. It seemed as though I was not concerned about the answer. I wouldn't be surprised if I was praying about the topic with the answer right before me. Someone out there might know what I am talking about. I am now more aware and intentional with my prayer points.

After all the praying you have done, I would like to say to you, "One of these days will be your day." You will be celebrated, you will see it, you will touch it, and you will possess it. Keep on praying and wait for you to happen. Remember, just because you have not seen it doesn't mean you won't possess it.

They that Are with Us Are More Than They that Are with Them (2 Kings 6:16)

12

WHEN YOU MAKE UP YOUR mind about going after your goal, sometimes it feels like no one is with you. You are all alone, and you seem to be the only one that understands you. It may seem difficult to see the support around you. It can appear as though you have no source of resources, encouragement, and motivation.

Your focus should be if God said it, then it is so. What it really means is as long as you are working on a God-approved project, you can stand.

Situations may arise, and circumstances may change. It may appear to alter what God told you to pursue. It can cause you to doubt.

Understand that these are called setbacks and stumbling blocks. Be lest assured they are not strong enough to stop you. To every good thing there is opposition. Your Job is to keep fighting until you get to that promised expected end.

Beware of the biggest obstacle called yourself. As much as you are the carrier of the vision be sure to do the work. Don't talk yourself out of doing something. This will come as a result of fear, discouragement, pitfalls, and allowing the enemy to whisper negativity in your ears.

In 2 Kings 6, the servant was terrified. He told the prophet Elisha that the army had surrounded the city. He asked, "What shall we do?" The prophet responded that they had more on their side than what he could see. Then he prayed for God to open the eyes of the servant to the unseen world. The scripture refers to the unseen world. This lets us know that there is an army in the unseen world fighting for us daily. Most assuredly we have Jesus who is ever interceding for us in heaven. If you have God on your side, you surely have more than enough to meet your goal.

It will take prayer for God to reveal to you what is to come, that will boost your confidence. That will be enough insight for you to move forward.

Beware that in the unseen world, there is also an army working against you. As much as you are not to fear that army, be aware that it can have an effect. This opposition is what you are pressing against as you chase after fulfilling the promise (your God-given goal).

I remember in one Bible study, we were talking about the supernatural. As we discussed, God began to reveal to me a deeper understanding of the supernatural. I realized at that time, the supernatural is not after all angels, demons, or spooky stuff. It's actually a world we get to tap into more than we think. When I looked up the meaning of the word *supernatural*, I read various definitions, and this one from Wikipedia stood out to me: "some force beyond scientific understanding or the laws of nature."

I remember reading the book of Daniel. In chapter 2, when King Nebuchadnezzar sent out a decree stating that if the wise men did not give the interpretation of his dream, he would kill them, Daniel heard of this and asked for time to seek from the Lord. God supernaturally revealed to him the interpretation of the king's dream. There is no easier way to explain how he got that knowledge because it was through a conversation with God using a technique we commonly refer to as prayer.

There are multiple ways we can engage in the supernatural. The supernatural is that unseen world which is known as the realm of the spirit. We can have a glimpse into this world by praying, reading the Word, visions, revelations, and through preaching of the Word.

First of all, I believe the act of engaging in prayer is already supernatural. I say that because we don't really see what is happening as we pray. I believe it's supernatural because when we pray, we exercise our faith which is not tangible. However, we believe something is happening and we do it anyway. Therefore, it's supernatural for one to engage in prayer without the 20/20 vision of the effect of it.

There are instances we pray at length, while others are shortened prayers; it is the sincere intent of the heart that will bring forth results.

Prayer can be targeted toward warfare, which can cause total chaos in the realms of the spirit. You can be strategic in your prayer by understanding your target. That's why one should never underestimate their prayer even though they can't see what is happening.

There are times when you have engaged in long-term prayers and are at a point where you feel exhausted, but the truth be told, there is not one word you have prayed that has not gone before the Lord. As you continue to pray about your need, you are building a bridge, and if you continue praying just a little longer, you will strengthen the bridge for others to walk on it as well. Things are happening in the supernatural. Keep building your bridge.

I once read that a Chinese bamboo tree, when planted, doesn't germinate out of the ground till after four years. In the fifth year, it grows up to ninety feet in just four to five weeks. The tree is believed to grow an average of forty inches a minute. You can actually see the tree grow.

My understanding is that a tree growing that tall spent four years extending its roots that anchored deep into the ground. The anchorage is what supports the weight and length of that bamboo tree. If you stay rooted and grounded in the Lord, your roots will grow deep enough to connect with the living water. Prayer will not be such a challenge as you will understand that in due season you shall reap.

What's interesting to me about this bamboo is that as it grows underground, no one can see it. Perhaps no one knows there is anything growing except the one who planted it. But as soon as it germinates, the tree is noticeable and unstoppable. I know this is about to be someone's testimony any day from now.

As your roots grow deeper, no one can see behind the scenes, but when you finally germinate, not everyone will understand the ground work and how long it took for you to be standing that tall. The one who created you knows what he planted, and he sees your end from your beginning. Remember the bamboo effect is applicable in your finances, church members, business, wisdom, scripture, employees, knowledge, understanding, and the list goes on and on. It is as a result of where you anchor yourself.

We have been challenged to pray without ceasing, and when you have been in prayer so long, you understand that there comes elevation. If only we could grasp the power and effectiveness of prayer, we would pray more.

There is a benefit in consistency in prayer. We call on a power that provides unseen assistance. We gain knowledge, wisdom, and understanding. We are cautioned that my people perish for lack of knowledge. Knowledge comes by hearing and hearing by the Word of God.

There are multiple events in the Bible where we've seen God supernaturally work:

He parted the Red Sea.

He impregnated a virgin without any involvement of sexual intercourse.

He walked on water and allowed Peter to do the same.

He turned water into blood.

He made a donkey speak.

And he made the lame man walk, the blind man see, and he called Lazarus back to life.

With all this evidence, there is no doubt that you are a part of this list.

Don't Underestimate You

13

IT IS VERY EASY TO overlook yourself based on your past experiences and/or failures.

You are more powerful than you think you are. Forget your past, it's already past, and forget your failures, they don't define you. You cannot get ahead by looking back. You are more than what you think of yourself. Even when you think highly of yourself, chances are that you can go higher than your current position. I say this from a humble perspective, not from a place of arrogance or pride. We know God detests pride. This is strictly coming from the perspective of endless and unlimited possibilities.

It doesn't come easy to think of yourself as a tool for change. Each one of us has various reasons. Reasons such as "I am too old, I am too young, I am too big, I am too small, I am way too tall or way too skinny, I don't have a degree, I was raised different, that's just how I am," and blah blah blah. It's an ongoing list, and we forget to utilize the priceless gifts within us. Gifts such as love, common sense, patience, kindness, respect, character, morals, manners, trust, gratitude, integrity, talents, and our right mind. You know what you have within you. Use it.

Start off with what seems or is easily attainable for you. The most important thing is that you decide and then do. To decide is not good enough, it should be accompanied by some action. As you accomplish goals, it builds your confidence and allows you to make bigger and creative goals. With positive results, you also realize that your state of mind changes. When that happens, your mind opens up to bigger and better. The more knowledge you accumulate, the increase in capacity of what your brain can retain and God will reveal more to you.

In Jeremiah 33:3, God has summoned us to call unto him and he will show us great and mighty things.

"Call unto me, and I will answer thee, and show thee, great and mighty things, which thou knowest not" (Jeremiah 33:3, KJV).

We have the right to call unto God for answers insight and understanding for what we don't understand.

The Bible says that we are transformed by the renewing of our minds.

"And be not conformed to this world: but be ye transformed by the renewing of your mind, that ye may prove what is good, and acceptable and perfect will of God" (Romans 12:2, KJV).

As knowledge is poured into you, you gain understanding which should bring forth change. This should lead you to hunger for more. At some point, you get to birth out what's already in you. These are things God has already implanted in you. He has been waiting on you to wake up and smell the coffee for him to work your gift in his best intent. What's so amazing about this is that you start to realize that you are more than capable. You can respond by pushing harder.

After you find out who you are and understand that sky is indeed the limit, remember to embrace the new you.

What's astonishing about doing God's will or having an obedient spirit is that you find out that you have already started the work that God wants you to do. You were just not aware.

Testimony

14

ONE EVENING AS I SPOKE to a good friend of mine, she mentioned that sometimes she doesn't understand when people say God talks to them, and if he does, she doesn't think he talks to her.

I proceeded to explain to her that sometimes it's because we complicate things by setting specific expectations. I shared a few examples of how he speaks to us through situations, other people, as well as our pastors, and through all kinds of channels. I let her know that she must be attentive. I gave her a book from my collection, *How to Listen to God* by Dr. Charles Stanley.

Before she left, I asked her to do an exercise with me. The exercise was for us to engage in prayer and then listen for a response from God. I told her to listen and not to think that whatever thought hits her mind is weird or could not be from God. After praying, we went into a moment of silence.

As we were listening, I heard the Lord say to me, "You will be a fisher of men, and you will feed a multitude of nations." I thought this was weird, and I had just warned my friend not to think that way. She shared her side of what she heard. I was hesitant about sharing mine because it was way off according to my mind, but I shared anyway. The word I received remained fresh in my mind except I had no idea what to do about it. Like many of us, I just assumed, well, I'm sure one day in the future it will make sense, and if anyone thinks as deep as I do, they would know that the future is not anytime soon.

Fast forward a month after the word had come to me, I contacted a friend who had mentioned to me that he has a passion for street ministry. He told me about how active he was when he lived in Texas. While in Idaho, he mentioned that he did it sporadically. I told him I was interested in going with him the next time he went out on his street ministry.

We agreed we would start the following Tuesday. When Tuesday came, we went downtown to a place where many homeless people were. It was a different experience for me as there were so many people under the influence of drugs, alcohol, depression, bitterness, anger, hatred. There was no way to tell what reaction I would get from such an environment. I was so scared as I thought some might have had guns, knives, or an aggressive attitude. It was very hard for me to ask questions or even interact, so instead, I listened to my friend as he interacted with them. I was so glad that I was wise enough to go with a man instead of a fellow female friend.

The next Tuesday, I was more relaxed and able to interact with more people. We usually never went empty-handed, so we quickly gained acknowledgment whenever we got there. We continued our visits on Tuesdays for a while. We ministered to all kinds of people in all sorts of places. Six months later, for the very first time, I had the opportunity to lead someone to Christ. At this time, the word I had heard when I was praying with my friend came alive. I realized it wasn't long before the word that God gave me manifested. All along I had been fishing, and I was not aware. We fed, clothed, and provided as God permitted. I felt that this ministry blessed me more that it may have blessed them.

The picture I'm painting is that you will subconsciously start fulfilling the word upon your life without knowing it. Nonetheless it will take that conscious effort to pursue.

Yes, some things will seem weird, but don't underestimate yourself. And yes, you will hear him correctly, and even though we try to tuck it away, at some point, the word must come alive and fully manifest.

Life is like a GPS; when you take the wrong turn, it recalculates as the destination is set. So whether we ignore God or not, at some point, we must get to where we need to go. We must start pursuing the things that are essential in our paths. Through experience, I learned that you cannot allow yourself to be complacent. Complacency can feel good or comfortable, but it's important to remind yourself that things could be better. This is a way for you to move from good to better and eventually greatness. If you want to succeed in anything you do, you must know that it takes hard work and consistent effort. Sometimes it hurts, but it's that pain that usually brings joy. You must undergo the pain in order to be successful.

Our now may not look good, but that can change tomorrow. Don't kill your dream. One thing I can continuously live to testify is if you are determined to see him work and show himself mightily, he sure will.

Once You Know, Then You Know

15

ONCE YOU KNOW WHAT YOU are supposed to do, there is no excuse not to do it. Once you know what you are capable of, there is no turning back.

It is beneficial to have moral courage, to make your actions consistent. You are your knowledge of right and wrong.

It has been said that ignorance is not an excuse. I break it down like this:

"My people are destroyed for lack of knowledge" (Hosea 4:6).

The Bible states that his people perish for lack of knowledge. This means ignorance does not qualify for an excuse. Just because you're not aware of what you're capable of does not give you a reason not to do what you are supposed to do. With that said, it's even more reason for you to use what you know as it will make room for you to know more. Basically accelerating/being in motion is the gateway to more. You can't risk situations where you claim ignorance as an excuse. This may cost you a lot more than you bargained for; if there is an option well attainable to protect yourself from the worst, it is to take possible action.

You are already aware of things that are ringing in your ears through different mediums. Mediums such as social media, television, conversation, devotionals, or through preachers. When you hear a message regardless of the medium, you may not understand that it's God giving you a message. Most of the time, God is confirming the very answer you have been looking for.

"[T]his is the third time I am coming to you. In the mouth of two or three witnesses shall every word be established" (2 Corinthians 13:1, NKJV).

The Word of God never lies and so let every man be a liar and God be the only truth. Confirmation is an indication that you are on track. It is the hope and encouragement to get started or continue the road you're on. It is the ammunition you need to face your giant.

Also remember that confirmation comes in many forms. Don't be looking for an answer that is familiar to you. Be open and alert. If it has been revealed to you, then it means it is attainable. Knowledge is key, and most importantly spiritual knowledge is extremely important in order to pursue the physical and theoretical knowledge. The Bible says,

"[W]here there is no vision, the people perish" (Proverbs 29:18a, KJV).

This lets me know when the vision has already been revealed, then it's only a matter of time before execution. Execution can take a long time from the initial time of the vision or the exact opposite. Things can turn around overnight. God is a miracle working God, and his power is unimaginable.

"Ah Lord God! Behold, thou has made the heaven and the earth by thy great power and stretched out arm, and there is nothing too hard for thee" (Jeremiah 32:17, KJV).

Yes, indeed, there is nothing too hard for the Lord. And the knowledge we already have, God gave it to us. It should normally be easier to trust him especially when we know that we know, that we know.

The bottom line is, we must use what we know now in order to gain more information to complete the journey.

How I Did It

16

IN THIS CHAPTER, I AM going to tell you a little bit of how I did everything I did or attempted to do what I wanted to do. Firstly, I want to thank my amazing pastor, Pastor Bryant Townsend, for always stressing a point that is very dear to my heart.

Every now and then, he talked about "When a woman makes up her mind…there's nothing that can stop her." I personally believe this is applicable to any person who sets their mind to get something done. But there's something very special about a woman that when she is determined to do what she wants to do, believe it will be done. I believe a woman was made with great inner instinct and power.

I had always wanted to be a business owner, but I couldn't get myself to make that decision. I felt like it was a farfetched idea. I told myself things such as I didn't have the finances to make it happen or that it wasn't the best time.

One day, I got a call from work (at the time I worked from home). The company manager informed me they were downsizing and had to let me go. I wasn't very surprised as they had already let go of so many employees. I knew it was only a matter of time before they would approach me. As soon as I was out of the job, I started looking for another job. In less than a week, I found another job. Between my old job and my newfound job, I never missed a pay check, and life continued. Three weeks into my new job, once again, I was told they were letting me go.

Every time I lost or quit a job, which is not that often, I never had to worry about my next move. Except this time, I was extremely hurt because I felt I was unfairly judged. Little did I know, God was steering me in a different direction. This is where my new journey began. Out of hurt and frustration, I vowed not to let someone determine whether I eat or what I eat. I decided I was going to pursue my business, but I had to pray to God to confirm which of the ideas I was to pursue. I felt the need to pursue my dream. I was still in a position of not knowing how I was going to start or whether I would have the resources. The difference this time was that I was determined to get some answers and direction from God. So I embarked on a journey of fasting and prayer, and he told me to pursue.

I remember getting off my knees on my last day of prayer and fasting, and literally my doorbell rang. It was my friend Susan. In conversation, Susan suggested that I apply for a grant. Immediately I set out to write a proposal to apply for the grant. I applied in December of 2014 and waited for the recipients to be announced in March of 2015. I was confident I was going to get the funds. In the meantime, I searched for a seasonal job while I waited. A block from my house was an accounting firm looking for an admin assistant, and there I was. I got hired from the January 15 and was to work to April 15 when tax season would be over. I would be right on time to launch my new business.

When March 12 came, I was granted $2,500. I wasn't awarded the entire amount of $7500 as I expected, but I still believed I was on to a great start. Once I received the money, I knew there was no turning back. I had prayed about it and promised that when the funds came, I would use the funds to start the business. From that day, I lost sleep. I thought about how, when, where, and what I was going to do next. It wasn't the easiest of experiences to go through. I had my business plan written out and most of my research done as much as I knew how. Again, plan, plan, and then plan some more.

Finally, I launched my hair business on April 25, 2015. That sounds straightforward, but it wasn't as easy as you are reading it. The process was very stressful accompanied with many sleepless nights. My brain was in constant operation even when I begged it to go to sleep. I worked long hours on the computer. Emails, calls, research—the list is endless. I had to make the little bit of money I had to work for me.

Keep in mind, when I was awarded the funds, a few months had already gone by from the time I set out to pursue the business. By this time, I wasn't as excited and motivated as I was before. I became terrified about going forward. However, my comfort and peace came from the fact that God had made a way. The things that needed to be done were above my knowledge, but I promised to make things happen, and so I did. I slowly started building my inventory and clientele. I closely watched my clients' demand and invested in that. I developed client relationships, networks, and things began to happen. I learned how to hustle and discovered I had quite a good hustle in me. I began to understand the intricacies of the hair industry. I took a trip to California to familiarize myself with the industry and operation techniques. I met new business contacts and mentors while in California. I acquired more inventory and began to grow my business.

While all this was going on, I had a side hustle working part time, from 12:00a.m. to 8:00a.m.

My sales were increasing, and the excitement was clear. Then I ran into a demand-and-supply issue. I didn't have enough cash on hand to restock as often. I decided to go look for another job specifically to supplement my business. September 4 of 2015, I interviewed for another part-time job with the department corrections. Everyone was impressed with me. I was hired on the spot and scheduled to start Monday, September 7.

On September 5, close to midnight, I received a dreadful phone call. This call would change my life as an upcoming entrepreneur. One of my peers called me and informed me that the marketplace building was on fire. I calmly told her to keep me informed. As soon as I hang up my phone, another peer called me. At this time, I was convinced that something was really wrong. He invited me to go with him to the market place. Lo and behold, all the stores were in flames.

I remember having no emotions at all as I watched the building burn down. When it was about two in the morning, I left the scene and said, "I've got to get some sleep. I have church early in the morning."

Monday came, and I went to my new job. My employer was so happy that she hired me and so sorry that my business was gone. After a week, my mind finally wrapped around my loss, and I broke down. Like I shared previously, I became depressed and unmotivated. Everything seemed to go sour at this point and while sour can be a pleasant taste at times that was not the case for me. I cried out to God, and I heard him once again say, "If you thought you had started, wait and see what's about to happen." I was assured that the fact that the business was birthed on my knees, that he would still make it come to pass. I looked forward to the beauty that was going to come out of those ashes.

In my time of misery, I stayed home in my bed, wondering what I was supposed to do. On the left side of my bed was a wall I called the wall of fame. I had pictures on that wall as reminders of things I aspire to do and want in life. I looked at my wall and thought to myself, *What is it on this wall that I can do right now?* The reason I thought of "right now" was because I had to get out of the headspace I was in. I knew there was something I could do right away.

After reviewing my wall of fame, I noticed I had goals to get my body in shape, grow my hair, play the piano, and much more.

As I write this book, I am still undergoing the process. I am not waiting for the perfect day or the perfect time. I am trusting God with every step of the way which in my case every page of the way. I type with his help and with the counsel of his wisdom.

There have been times I read through this book, and my own book ministers to me. I know that there have been many times I have written under the anointing of the Holy Spirit.

Just to reiterate, when I first started writing this book, I had a timeframe for the book to be done, but in the process, I realized that I couldn't write as planned. At some point, I knew I had to yield to the outpour of his word. I quickly recognized when it was happening. If I wasn't near my computer, I would store memos on my phone or a piece of paper. And that is how this book came together. I share all this to say: start where you are with what you have available to you right now.

As you take your steps, you will gain momentum, and at some point, you will start running. I know that some individuals think that the hardest part of any project is maintaining it or sustaining it. I beg to differ. I believe the hardest part is getting started. And yes, there are some people who start but don't finish, but I say if you are able to start, you sure do have the capability to finish. When I got started, I saw five pages, then I saw nineteen pages, forty-five pages, and then I saw sixty-eight pages. I realized this could easily turn into two hundred pages. Every step you take is a step closer to your goal. You have to have a goal, and you have to believe in it.

I went through some difficult and challenging times, but that didn't stop me. As a matter of fact, it made me want to work even harder. I had to overcome. I had to keep moving, and I had to keep pressing even when I had friends and loved ones who either didn't believe in me or mocked me.

I still had those who knew that I was a volcano about to erupt (in a good way). With or without support, I had to make it through. I was very aware it wasn't going to be an easy journey, but I also knew that it was a journey I had to take. The only one who needed to be convinced to take this journey was myself. I pressed and I pressed and I continue to press because there is a benefit to pressing. It's just like praying without ceasing. And as I look back now, I know that every bit of what I have been through was essential to the process. If it was easy to do anything, then we would all do it. And the truth is we all can do it but only if you are willing to persevere.

You may not want to go through anything, but God has a way to intervene and push you toward the path you must take. You might start off like me, who doesn't like to deal with trials and tribulations but ends up embracing each one of them. I recognized what each one of them represented. It doesn't always feel good, but it is for the greater good. God does nothing without purpose, and now, it's easier for me to go through trials because I understand that "this too shall pass."

I am not saying that I am excited about trials or that I am all smiles while I am going through, no. I am saying that as I go through, I have it in the back of my mind that it's just for a moment. My reaction can be anything from frustration, tears with lots of prayer, and sometimes just lots of tears. At times it turns into sleepless nights, isolation, and the list goes on and on.

I try my best not to wallow in it for a long time. I really don't like entertaining misery. It doesn't feel good. Half the time, it magnifies the problem. Be careful not to misunderstand the process. What was meant to push you into better might be misinterpreted into God is out to get you or is punishing you. You might end up in the "woe me" attitude.

Don't be afraid to be vulnerable. In order to trust completely, in order to overcome pride, in order to truly speak out of your heart, you will have to be vulnerable. Do not be ashamed to ask for prayer. Do not be afraid to ask for help. Do not be prideful in asking for whatever resources you might need in order to put together your project. Your project maybe ministry, singing, dancing, writing, a business, a class, your children, your marriage, or whatever it is that you need. Learn to ask, seek, knock, and the door shall be open unto you.

I know nowadays we are living in a world that people just don't open up. Christians seem to be growing apart more and more because we have beliefs that Christians are very judgmental. That's a whole another book. Coming soon!

Regardless what your view is, God is willing to bless anyone who is willing to work at what they want. He said faith without works is dead. Get up and go after that "thing" one more time.

I dare you to dream again.

I dare you to live again.

I dare you to pick up from where you left off.

Some of you, it's just a matter of releasing the pause button. You need to resume. And some of you are at a place where you need to get within yourself and figure out what this project is. However, for most of you, you already know what you want to do, but you worry about the whos, hows, whens, and wheres. My words of encouragement to you are "Start anyway."

You started, and somehow, you stopped, but guess what? You can continue or start again.

You thought about it, and it was scary to execute. Execute, anyway.

You started, it was going great, and something hit along the way and now you are having no hope. You are actually in a better position because you've seen it work before. You know what to do different. With all the time you put into it the first time, your work is already cut out for you.

My Parents

17

MY PARENTS WERE QUITE A pair, I must say. My mother was very beautiful, and my dad till this day remains handsome. Yes, the truth be told.

My mum passed when I was just twenty years old, and I say just because anyone who has a relationship with their mother knows that the older you get, the more you need your parents, and vice versa. I don't know if anyone can relate to that good feeling when your parents think you are old enough for them to confide in you. I can vividly recall just how good it felt when my mother at one time needed my advice.

My mother had such a great spirit of determination. She was ever determined to do a whole lot, and more importantly, she was an overcomer. There were so many things that my mother accomplished. I know that it wasn't that someone encouraged her to do it, but it was more so that she had so much opposition around her, telling her she couldn't do it. She looked back at opposition and said, "I will thrive," and she did. She turned that story around into a story that many of us live to tell. And every time I feel weary or faint and look back at my mum's story, I know that all things are possible. I am persuaded that if my mum was still alive, her story would be great, but I am determined to do greater. I will never forget that I am a seed birthed out of the womb of a determined overcomer. I have just as much capacity to overcome—better yet, I have a greater work to accomplish. There are projects Mama didn't accomplish, but through me she will. I have projects of my own that combination calls for greater works.

My dad on the other hand, like most fathers, was a firm believer of providing and protecting his children. He gave us anything and everything we needed. Sometimes, he even went an extra mile providing what we didn't need or perhaps didn't know we needed.

What I want to point out is, as a child who grew up knowing that I could ask my dad for anything I needed, at some point, I took that for granted.

What I want to stress about this is "Parents, don't give so much money to your kids." And by "so much" money, I am referring to the actual cash in their hands. This is another chapter of its own, but I'll touch a little bit on why it is significant.

I always had cash given to me. I felt the need to always have it because it was possible to have it whenever I needed it. As much as I felt the need to have it, I never pursued a way to make the cash myself. Somehow, I thought my dad had a tree where he plucked the money from. In the process, I missed out on the opportunity to learn those skills earlier in life. The good news is I eventually learned. It was such a tough process for me to transition from Daddy's little girl into adulthood, but God did it! Remember this: you are never too old, too young, too skinny, too big, too short, too tall. Change can take place when you make up your mind that you want to see change.

Don't get me wrong, providing for your children is good, but make sure you also teach them life skills. Prepare them for the real world. They must at some point fall in love with becoming a provider for themselves and others. They must learn or else they might resent adulthood. My dad's original intent was to make sure that we never go without. He was making sure we never had to seek from unwanted sources. He wanted to be that perfect example of a provider in our lives. He always told us that under his roof, we would never suffer or lack anything, and that remains true to this day.

When life became challenging for me, it was outside his roof. It's called adulthood.

Growing up, I couldn't tell you if we were born-again or not, but I can tell you that we went to church Sunday after Sunday without fail. As for me, chances are that I had accepted Christ many times. I didn't quite understand what I was doing. For every time I attended a service not in my church but in a setting such as student gatherings like Chi-Alpha, Scripture Union, I always responded to every salvation altar call. I had no idea it was a onetime deal lol.

After so many encounters of alter calls, my life with God started taking shape. With the little understanding I had, I prayed for my entire family. I just couldn't imagine what would happen to them if they didn't accept Christ. When it came to praying for my father, I felt like heaven would have to come down. Today that story is different, and I might just be right to say my father prays more than any other member of my family.

My father has always been a man of very few words, and growing up, those few words would make your day or mess your day. Whenever Dad said something, whether he yelled or asked you to do something politely, it always carried more weight than if Mama did. Most of us can relate to this. Chances are that Mama says it all the time, you get tired of hearing it. In Dad's case, it was a once-in-a-while deal, and it always had an impact.

Today my dad being a pastor is amazing because he is the most encouraging man I know in my life right now. For every situation I face and I present it to him, he always has the best words along with scripture to soothe me, and for that I am forever thankful.

Every time he says, "It will be all right," I can trust and believe that it will be all right.

There's something about a man and his authority that God naturally designed for men to be the vessel of. I believe that is why a woman is required to submit to him. A man was naturally made a leader, and any man who accepts to walk in his leadership will surely lead a multitude.

My dad's background is military/engineer/computer science. He didn't interact with us that much. You know how military disciplines can be at times. He didn't have much to say unless he was helping you with your homework, which usually meant you had done so bad in your math.

Sometimes it was a moment when you were telling him about what you were required to do in school or what was needed for school.

Our household was filled with more females than males, so you can imagine what that was like. All of us never talked to him about boyfriends or girlfriends. It was just a no-go topic toward him. This was not so because he said so. It was so because it just happened to be so. I look back and am quite thankful that was the case. I can't imagine having to talk about each relationship I've been in. I believe it's more important to me to introduce someone to my father as the final product, if you know what I mean. I am of the belief that it's better to have the introduction once, instead of bringing a bunch of jokers every other year or however many times I have had to switch.

In my adulthood, I found it easier to approach him with stories about who I am dating, even though I still don't go into too much detail.

When I was in my last serious relationship, I called him, and I said I was seeing someone, that I was in love, and it was serious. I never told him the name, age, who he was, where he was from, or what he did.

My dad never bothered to ask either. I am pretty sure he thought, *Well, when you guys are ready, I'll eventually know more.* Here is why I appreciate that we never established that kind of a relationship.

Fast forward into this amazing relationship, I had to go back and tell him it was no longer that amazing. I felt just as responsible to let him know that this relationship was no more. It was a very difficult thing for me to do as I was dreading the question "What happened?" It's obvious. Anytime you have to share with a loved one about how a man is not treating you right, there is always some tension against that individual. What happens when you guys decide to patch up is that they are still stuck on the bad taste. So I prayed that he doesn't ask me that question, and he didn't. This is what he said instead: "Ecclesiastes 3." That was it. As I mentioned, a man of very few words but very impactful.

When I lost my business, he sent me scripture after scripture and heartfelt words of comfort and encouragement, and if my father on earth is so concerned about me, what more my Father in heaven?

When I started my business, he was there to encourage me.

When I was sick, he prayed for me, and that was the very first time I ever heard him pray ever in my life.

Sometimes I tend to forget all the things God has done for me, but putting this in writing causes me to repent. I can't thank God enough for an amazing father he saw fit to oversee my well-being on this earth.

I share this because it is important to acknowledge the good people in your life that you either look up to, can relate to, and encourage you all the way.

When They Say You Can't
and *He* Says You Can

~~~~~~~~~~~~~~~~~~~~~~~~~~~~~~~~~~~~~

18

You will be faced with a lot of opposition including your own self being the biggest one. The main piece of the puzzle is you. If you are convinced that he said it, then you can, so get it done.

When the going gets tough, take a breather and check in with your support crew, whether it's your peers, children, or your prayer warriors. I personally asked for prayer all the time. I had my "personal person" who always revived me when I was down.

All things work together for your good. I know of situations and circumstances I have been told, "This would never work out" or "This will never come to pass," and it's all coming together now. If I had listened to the negativity around me or even allowed myself to be discouraged by my own negative and fearful thoughts, I wonder where I would be today.

There will be instances where you must be okay with keeping to yourself. Sometimes the more you share your plans, the more you face opposition, discouragement, and negativity.

The other thing is, as crazy an idea may seem in your own mind, remember that it probably sounds worse in someone else's mind. This goes to show you everything you want to pursue should not be shared.

In some cases, God will send you the right people to connect with. If you feel the need to run it by someone, do so. Make sure it is someone you know will be supportive or someone who will give you solid advice that does not detract from your idea, project, or plan.

"*[F]or we wrestle not against flesh and blood, but against principalities, against powers, against the rulers of the darkness of this world, against spiritual wickedness in high places*" (Ephesians 6:12, KJV).

Understand that there will always be someone to tell you that you can't. If they don't tell you, they are probably thinking it. I'll break it down in two parts. If you are an individual who is trying to accomplish something, by all means do it. If you're the type of person that struggles to think outside the box or think big, be cautious in what you say as you may discourage someone.

If you are a parent who is still stuck in the "old ways," do not kill your children's dreams. Just because you have not come to that understanding of the current ways or technologies does not mean their ideas are not valid. Trust your children. They may be more knowledgeable about technology today. Pray for them, probe, and support them.

Do not be quick to speak against someone's dreams or ideas. Just because you tried it, and it failed, doesn't mean it's impossible for the other person to thrive. Instead share your experience, what you learned, and help them where you can.

If you are a parent that does not understand the idea your child discusses with you, try and learn something.

It's sad to say that some parents today are living with regrets of trying to impose things on their children. They try to relive their lives through their children, so they tell them what to do. What happens is, when the child finally reckons with their path, they later have resentment as they did not pursue their passion.

Give your children a chance to figure out things on their own. If it's dancing they love, let them dance. If it's singing, let them sing. Don't try to make them a lawyer when in fact they would rather sing.

I know a young man in college that quit pursuing a degree in medicine and is venturing into establishing his own business. He has not informed his parents yet as he is afraid they will be disappointed. Being of African descent, I know many parents who wouldn't even look at this young man's situation from his point of view. They wouldn't put into account his heart's desire. To them, they consider this a disgrace to the family. They have forgotten to put him first and give him the opportunity to choose.

Parents, friends, and loved ones can say you can't. If your heart and mind are determined with everything that you are to achieve that goal, you can. You and me both believe that you can.

There may be a time that you may be walking in the shoes of what your parents want you to be or what other people want you to be/think you should be. This likely happens because you never had the opportunity to choose or perhaps you didn't know any better. Your parents or someone of influence in your life may have imposed it on you. Don't get me wrong, sometimes your parents know just what you need. In some instances, the choices they make for you work because they help you find yourself, but in some cases, they are oblivious to your heart's desire.

The important thing is once you feel you have found your way and passion, make sure to be firm in your decision and pursue.

There is a way to respectfully decline something that is being imposed on you. Sometimes being stagnant means you are listening to every other voice other than God's. Be prepared to shift some people and friends around. If going for your passion means going against your parents (I know that's a tough one), don't worry about it, most parents love their children.

As much as they may feel that you have gone against them, once you make something out of your passion, they will soon accept and respect your decision. No one but you can prove the passion you have towards something. If you can't stand for it, then no one will. When you finally venture into something you love, you become the voice for those who are still struggling with their next step.

Become an encourager of good and positive influence to someone. God will continue to raise the same kind of people in your own life. When you fall, get up and keep pushing. Never view your failure as the end. The true end to anything you are pursuing is death. And even that is debatable. Some people have been more beneficial dead than alive.

As long as you are alive, you still have a chance to overcome. You also have the ability to pass the torch on. You still have a chance to achieve. The opportunity to create change and be that vehicle for change is still open to you.

The world is anxiously waiting for you. With such great talent you have, share it. You are more than a conqueror, and the best is yet to come. At this point in your life, you can only get better. There is no turning back. You are more than meets the eye. Be of good courage. You have already overcome.

Don't allow people to make you lose your vision. If you are going to walk in victory, you will have to prepare for a victorious life. If you lose anything or someone along the way, know that God wants better for you. Strive to walk and thrive in the most difficult and sometimes dangerous situations. You can do it!

My Spiritual Parents

19

THE TOWNSENDS ARE A MATCH from heaven, and they go by their first names Tanisha (Lady T, first lady) and Bryant (Pastor B). They have a lovely daughter called Joy Townsend.

I found it fitting to write about how they have been such a huge part of my spiritual growth. They helped build my confidence and zeal to go after anything I want to do. Sunday after Sunday was a word of encouragement.

There were times I could not hold a conversation without having to refer to what my pastor says or what he has taught me. And knowing it all to be nothing but the true Word of God is such a blessing.

When I first joined the church, I had different views about so many things, and some of it was just lack of knowledge. My pastor did an amazing job giving me/us different perspectives on things. That helped shape my life tremendously.

Every time someone would ask me who my favorite preacher was, I would contemplate on how hard it is to make a choice. There are many anointed people of God who are unique in their own way and so I would go through a list of names. But today I can honestly and wholeheartedly say my favorite preacher is my pastor, Pastor Bryant Townsend of Agape Christian Worship Center in Boise, Idaho.

My reasons are as follows:

He is the preacher that has tirelessly poured into my life, and I have seen myself transform.

I have never seen anyone with as much force of energy as my pastor. Even when he is tired, by the grace of God, he will deliver 110 percent.

His wisdom is out of this world. He is anointed. We are so blessed.

His humor is hilarious.

He is so real sometimes I wonder how many lives he has lived. His knowledge of the different aspects of life whether it's from a female's standpoint, male, young, or old, he just knows how to engage us all.

Our very own first lady is like no other. I personally refer to her as "the first, the one, the only."

As beautiful and classy as a doll, the word flows flawless through her. There couldn't have been a better match for my pastor. And of course my pastor is able to do all he does because of the great support that his great woman provides. You know what they say: behind a great man is a great woman.

My favorite times are the Sundays when they play what I call "tag team," and by that I mean, when my pastor preaches, and we find ourselves in a position I consider "set on fire" and hands the microphone to Lady T who "pours kerosene" to the flames. I can't describe it any better.

This is not the norm, but when it happens, I melt in admiration of what a great team God has blessed my life with.

My spiritual parents are anointed. If it was left up to me, I would have them anoint and pray over anything and everything that belongs to me. I mean including my pots, pans, and plates. Lol this is not to say I am one of those lazy members who cannot pray over their own stuff and just depend on the pastor for everything, no.

This is me recognizing the blessing of Agape Christian Worship Center and acknowledging the importance of the mantle upon the church. I know the Word says the angel of the house carries our blessings through the Word, laying of hands, and just by mere reverence of the man of God he is. It is my pleasure to take and exhaust as much as I can of what is before me. I am very blessed to have the Townsends as my spiritual parents.

At the beginning of 2015, they had declared, "The year of the extraordinary." The title in itself is exciting, and as I write this, today being October 30, 2015, I am looking back at how many things I have done out of the ordinary thus far. Writing this book is nothing I thought I would ever do. To top up, first lady says, "When you start living the extraordinary life, you can't go back." I am looking forward to more surprises for myself. I am learning how to balance my extraordinary living. I am balancing both spiritually and physically. It is my desire to go the extra mile in all that I do.

Once again, I would like to express a special thank you to my spiritual Parents. The least I can do to show my gratitude is to always remember to lift them up in prayer for the priceless work their lives are committed to. I would also like to encourage someone out there to honor your leaders. There is a blessing in that. Remember to cover them in prayer. They are just as human as you are, and they go through the same emotions we go through. They face more opposition, it's only fair we pray for them as they pray for us.

You Are Almost There

―――――――――‿∾◦⊶⊕⊶◦∾‿―――――――――

20

I ALSO WANTED TO ENCOURAGE you: if you have read this far, it means you have grasped the concept. My prayer is that you believe in yourself enough to decide and then do.

Many of us in one sense or another are confident that we can pinpoint one, two (for some of us), three, or more things that we know are waiting to be done. Not only are these things/goals waiting to be accomplished, you also understand and know that God wants them accomplished through you.

One of the fears I had when I was down was the thought that if I didn't get up and do something, nothing was going to be done, and I would waste away. Worse off, the project I had birthed would be nonexistent unless I turned my breakdown into a breakthrough. In my down time, I'd rally myself up in imagination, confidence, excitement, and motivation. I was determined that while I waited, I would be productive. Eventually, I gathered enough strength to get back to work on the word that God had given me.

I present to you: *What Can I Do?* This is the book you are reading.

I must say time can become the enemy of your faith, but as you read this book, I pray you have figured it out or are figuring it out. You are truly almost there. If you keep pushing, you will soon conquer. Some of you don't need that much pushing. You already know what to do, including when you are going to start.

Every new day is one step closer to your goal.

If you started, finish! If you haven't started, start! It's never too late. If you started and then stopped, start again, or better yet, pickup from where you left. If you don't know what to do yet, you are not alone. We all didn't know what to do at some point nor how to.

What is your inner voice telling you right now? Yes, you! Stop and listen. Yep, that's it! Now start, continue, and then finish. If you think it's too late to start, it's better late than never. If you think you're too old to start, you'll still be old with just an idea or a dream, and nothing to show for it. I mean if you are forty-five, and you know that it takes at least ten years to better your project, if you start now, in ten years you will be fifty-five and successful. Or you can choose not to start and still turn fifty-five with only regrets of "I wish" to show for. The choice is yours. What kind of a fifty-five-year-old do you want to be?

Remember that every day you invest time into your project is progress. It's a step closer to where you ought to be.

You must keep pressing, pushing, and believing. Sometimes you will call into existence what is not, but the more you believe it, the more it becomes.

They say, "The difference between successful people and unsuccessful people is that successful people do what unsuccessful people don't want to do."

You must be willing to do more than you are doing right now. You have got to be uncomfortable at times. Be prepared to be hurt, to be criticized, and to feel like quitting; that's all part of the process. Do not give up because you are almost there.

It Is Finished

21

Yes, THE BOOK IS FINISHED, and you just read it ha-ha-ha. This is the end of this book, but the beginning of a whole new chapter of my life. This magnifies my life as an author and the very next chapter of my life. The secret is, if you make up your mind to get something done, go after it with everything you've got. *You can do it.* Whether it's a sport, ministry, marriage, business, or life decisions, it will work for you. Sometimes it starts off with a specific idea, and it turns into a whole other blessing. You find that one road that merges into the highway, and when you get to the highway, you need to increase your speed.

You must keep up with the rest of the speeding traffic going in your direction but yet different destinations. On this highway are different cars with different horse power engines and capabilities. Some are fast cars, some are newer models, some are old models, and some more reliable than others. The drivers of these cars come from different backgrounds, have unique personalities, and are of different age groups. We are all different individuals moving at our own paces. Everybody that's willing is able on this journey.

Start that business, join that gym, study one extra hour, tarry three more hours in that prayer. Dare to dream for you will not die but live to declare the goodness of the Lord. Put your hands to the plough; in due season, you shall soon reap.

God bless you all the way through the journey you about to embark on.

About the Author

BORN AND RAISED IN ZAMBIA (south central of Africa), Charlotte was always that girl that wanted to do more. At a very young age, she mastered the art of entrepreneurship. Her grandmother had always told her she had a business acumen, but she would only realize this for herself after she completed her undergraduate years. In her own words, "Business is a form or method to transform an idea, gift, or talent into money or worth," she says this as she laughs.

She obtained two degrees one in business and the other in marketing. Since then, her ideas in business have been innumerable. Sometimes, she has ideas that have her friends thinking, *That's wonderful but challenging*. Charlotte understands that the only person she must prove to that she can do it is herself. She owes her all to fulfilling her passion while impacting the rest of the world around her positively.

Charlotte is a firm believer of "You can do it" as long as your mind, spirit, and body are in agreement. Even when the three are misaligned, one must still move forward.

She continues to explore the various ways and forms to keep her business "sense" alive. Her explosive mind of ideas is warmly embraced by friends and family. She continues explore and connect through faith, strength, loss, beauty, self-worth, love, healing, prayer, and forgiveness. She hopes to continue this expression for years to come.

CPSIA information can be obtained
at www.ICGtesting.com
Printed in the USA
LVHW032300110720
660354LV00006B/608

9 781641 915960